e MyBook
http://mybook.egeaonline.it

Type your username and password or register by clicking on **Create a new account**.

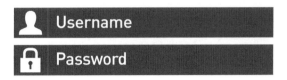

| Username |
| Password |

In MyBook you can access the accompanying resources (both text and multimedia),
the **BookRoom**, the **EasyBook** app and your purchased books.

CODE

> **PYTHON2019**

Type the code in the **Activation Code** field

MY PURCHASED BOOKS

ENTER YOUR CODE   Activation code [   ] >

The code must be typed only the fi st time you access **MyBook**
and cannot be used thereafter.

PYTHON
FOR NON-PYTHONIANS
How to Win over Programming Languages

Gaia Rubera
Francesco Grossetti

EGEA S.p.A.
Via Salasco, 5 - 20136 Milan, Italy
Phone + 39 02 5836.5751 - Fax +39 02 5836.5753
egea.edizioni@unibocconi.it - www.egeaeditore.it

First edition: February 2019

ISBN Domestic Edition 978-88-99902-41-4
ISBN International Edition 978-88-85486-86-7
ISBN Pdf Edition 978-88-85486-87-4

Contents

Preface

Whether or not you are familiar with the world of programming languages, you would probably know that there are currently hundreds of them. They can serve very different goals and their characteristics might change quite dramatically.

We can be sure about one thing, though: developing the correct mindset to start using one of these languages is fundamental in order to solve complex real-world problems. Whether we have to deal with remote databases or with Social Media data, being able to access and manipulate the information contained in this data is a key competitive advantage in today's world.

The goal of this book is to give you an easy access point to start exploring the vast world of programming languages. In particular, in this manuscript we focus our attention on one of the most common and versatile languages, called Python.

The book uses a very simple and accessible language. All the descriptions of Python features come with intuitive examples to make you learn by doing. This is not a theoretical book and does not cover some of the most internal features of Python. The intention of the authors is to allow business oriented people to start using Python. The main reason for such a choice of style is due to the increasing number of requests by non-technical professionals to solve daily problems and tasks. Whether we want to append multiple spreadsheets or profile the customer base, being able to use a solid infrastructure which enables to collect, check, process, analyze data, and report results has become a basic requirement in most industries.

This work starts with a brief introduction to the Python language by presenting some of its most important features. We will learn how to install Python and how to start talking with it through different front-ends. We will then begin to define objects and to recognize their different characteristics and features. Each section ends with a few exercises to make the reader comfortable with the concepts just introduced.

This book comes with an online version available at http://mybook. egeaonline.it. The online version cannot be downloaded but it is a color version to facilitate code reading.

Acknowledgements

We are enormously indebted to Francesco Balocco, a Research Assistant at Bocconi University in 2013, who first introduced us to Python. The most engaging exercises in this book are his. We would also like to thank the many students that, over the years, took the Social Media Marketing course offered at Bocconi University. Their feedback, and struggles, were instrumental in refining the material that ended up in this book. A big thank you to Aulona Ulqinaku and Federica Rossetti for fastidiously taking notes during class and providing the backbone of the book.

Finally, we would like to thank the Bocconi MBA Class of 2018, which was brave enough to demand the first Python course (The fact that they asked for it in addition to their normal course load makes their request even more exceptional.). Their request validated our intuition that Python (and, in general, programming) is no longer a technical add-on, but an essential tool for today's managers.

Chapter 1

Introduction

1.1 What is Python?

There are plenty of ways which we could begin this section with. We decided that a straightforward approach to understand what Python is, is to start with a clear and formal definition. So let's borrow it from the official website python.org.

> "*Python is an interpreted, object-oriented, high-level programming language with dynamic semantics.*"

Now, this is a very clear definition for anybody who is already familiar with all the concepts used in the definition itself. This book though, targets a different audience with potentially no expertise at all on programming languages, so we will go over the concepts mentioned in the definition.

Let's start with a very general point of view. Python is a programming language which is very flexible and adapts to different context. Whether you need a rapid development of applications up to large scientific projects which require intense computations, this language has your back. One of Python's main characteristics is that it is easy to learn since its syntax generally facilitates the readability of the code. Also, users love the fact that in many situations the syntax required to develop a given set of instructions resembles the plain English which makes Python formidable in terms of immediate understanding of its features.

One of the other peculiarity which we must take into account when are choosing a programming language is its flexibility and the capacity of being extended to increment its features. This job is carried out by the so called *modules*. We reserve a specific section of this book to modules since they play a very important role in code development.

On last important characteristic is that Python is a multi-platform environment. Whether we are using Windows, MacOS or any of the Linux distributions, the Python interpreter can always be installed and used.

It really seems that this is the language to learn, but remember? We have to understand a bit of how it works internally. In the following sections, we briefly cover some of the most important characteristics mentioned in the definition.

1.2   Compiled vs Interpreted

Do you remember when we started this book? One of the first things we said was about how many programming languages have been developed over time. The point is: can we classify all those languages? Is there a way to group a given language by referring to a specific characteristic? Of course, the answer to all these questions is yes, we can. For instance, one of the most important distinctions you can have is whether a programming language is a *compiled* or an *interpreted* language. Let's try to understand the main differences since these two families have different purposes as well as pros and cons.

A compiled language is one where the program has to be converted into machine readable code. We write the so called *source code* and then through a compiler we compile the source code to convert it and express the instructions into the readable code by the target machine. For example, an addition operation + in your source code could be translated directly to the ADD instruction in machine code. In terms of advantages, we sure have faster performance. This is ensured by the fact the we can use the native code of the targeted machine. Also, compiled languages offer quite powerful optimization during the compiling phase.

An interpreted language is one where the instructions are not directly executed by the target machine, but instead are read and executed by some other computer program called *interpreter* (which normally is written in the language of the native machine). For example, the same + operation would be recognized by the interpreter at run time and it would then call its own add(a,b) function with the appropriate set of instructions which would then execute the machine code ADD instruction. In terms of advantages, these languages are easier to implement. The reason is given by the fact that developing efficient (i.e. good) compilers can be very hard. For those of you who have some kind of familiarity with compilers, just think about the L^AT_EX compiler which is incredibly slow. The other good thing is that we do not need to run any compilation whatsoever. In other words, we can execute code directly "on the fly". Lastly, they are definitely more convenient for dynamic languages.

1.3   Object-Oriented Programming

Object-Oriented Programming (OOP) is a programming language model organized around *objects* rather than actions and *data* rather than logic. Historically, a program has been viewed as a logical procedure that takes input data, processes it, and produces output data. OOP takes the view that what we really care about are the objects that we have defined in our work space. We want to manipulate those objects rather than arguing about the underline logic required to manipulate them.

In OOP, objects play a major role then. They are the first things you think about when designing a program. Moreover, they can also be the result of the program you are developing. In other words, we work all the time with objects: we manipulate them to achieve a given data structure or a given result, for instance.

Objects can also be grouped into even conceptually higher and more abstract structures called *classes*. We will talk about classes later on in the book, so for now, let's think about them as a way to have objects which belong to the same class to share some characteristics. Each object can be seen as an instance of a particular class. Each class possesses its own methods or procedures and variables which call all be applied to whatever object belongs to the given class.

1.4   High-level Programming Language

A *high-level* language is a programming language designed to simplify computer programming and the life of the coder. The reason we refer to this class of languages with the term "high-level" is because of the level of abstraction and the simplification associated with it. A high-level language is far away from machine code which is understood by the internal processor of a computer.

In general, these type of languages have source codes which contain easy-to-read syntax, often almost in plain English. It is only at a later stage that instructions are converted in a language which can be read by a processor.

This is a fundamental aspect since it allows the coder to write complex algorithms using a *very* intuitive language (i.e. syntax). To give you a taste, this is what you need to do to print the string "Hello World" in Assembly, a well known low-level programming language very close to the machine code, and in Python which is a high-level language.

```
print('Hello World')
## Hello World
```

```
01
02  ; You may customize this and other start-up templates;
03  ; The location of this template is c:\emu8086\inc\0_com_template.txt
04
05  org 100h
06
07  ; add your code here
08
09  mov ah, 9      ;output string
10  mov dx, offset msg  ;Place address of msg variable reference into dx for str to print
11  int 21h        ;Execute interrupt call to print the string
12
13  mov ah, 8      ;Value 8 into ah, sub-function to wait for character input (pause)
14  int 21h        ;Execute Interupt call
15  int 20h        ;Exit com file
16
17  msg db "hellow world! $"
18
19  mov ah, 4ch
20  int 21h
21
22  ret         |
```

FIGURE 1.1: An example of program to print "Hello World" in Assembly.

As we can see, the effort is much less when using a high-level language such as Python. All we have to do to print the message `Hello World` is to invoke a built-in function called `print()`. For those readers who have already some kind of familiarity with Python might be aware of the recent update in its interpreter. Indeed, from Python 3.x.x the print method has become a function which we call with `print()`. In older versions, namely 2.x.x, the call was `print 'string to print'`. This book uses the more recent Python 3.x.x.

1.5   Static vs Dynamic Semantics

Let's start by thinking about the meaning of the two words: static and dynamic. Intuitively, something that is static does not change, while a dynamic entity of some sort has some probability to change over time. Also, we feel that something that is static would tend to be less flexible than something that is dynamic.

In computer science, this difference plays a major role and it affects the way we interact with the language we decided to adopt. Below, we briefly provide some intuitions about the difference between the two paradigms and their pros and cons.

One good starting point to distinguish the two is to consider the static semantic as an external world that represents the text of the program we are writing. This world does not change, hence the the label *static*. The dynamic semantic can be considered as the inner world that represents the hardware status (i.e. memory) at run-time. This world does change, hence the label *dynamic*. Effectively, it is where all happens and where the program gets executed.

Static objects are formal constructs in the code. They can be expressions, statements, structures and so on. In other words, they have no meaningful existence beyond compile-time. Dynamic objects instead are instances of values contained in those objects, locations and so on and thus they do exist at run-time level since the user interacts with these manifestations. One can now start asking what kind of interaction, if any, does exist between these two objects. A link between the worlds is called *binding* which is direct consequence of declaration. This allows us to easily build interactions between static objects and their dynamic counterparts.

One other fairly important concept is the *environment*. Both static and dynamic objects have their own environments. These incorporate all the knowledge about the objects that are defined and are aware of all the possible other relevant objects, both static and dynamic. In particular, the static environment must include what is known about each identifier from its declaration. In fact, the static environment maps each identifier to its type and the kind of declaration it came from. The static environment is invariant over time, but varies according to position within the program text. The dynamic environment relates identifiers to the dynamic objects that will be around at run-time. In other words, it maps each identifier to information about constants or variables or operations and so on. It will vary over time, as the program runs simply because there will be different objects at each point in time during the execution of the program itself.

One of the most impressive advantages of a dynamic semantics is the ability to bind a name to objects of different types and to do this at run-time (i.e. during the execution of the program). In the following example, we show how the name `my_object` is assigned an integer value (i.e. an integer type) and then a string value (i.e. a string type).

```
my_object = 9
my_object = "Hello World"
```

In a statically-typed language, the above sequence of statements is illegal. The reason is due to the static nature of the environment in which we define the objects. If an object (`my_object`) had been declared to be an integer, then this object cannot be changed at later times. In a dynamically-typed language this sequence of instructions is perfectly fine. As we can see below, we can ask Python to print the value of the object as well as the type. Type is a fairly new concept which will be discussed in details in later Sections. For now, it is a way to distinguish between different objects.

```
my_object = 9
print(my_object)
## 9
print(type(my_object))
## <class 'int'>
my_object = "Hello World"
print(my_object)
## Hello World
print(type(my_object))
## <class 'str'>
```

1.6   Installing Python

Python is a multi-platform software which typically comes pre-installed in Unix-like systems[1], like Linux and MacOS, but has to be explicitly installed in Windows systems.

Regardless of the operating system, in order to work with Python we need to have a Python interpreter. Once again, this book uses Python 3.x.x interpreter. There are a number of different ways in which we can download and install the interpreter. Below is a list of the main methods:

- *Python Software Foundation*: Python can be obtained from the official website Python.org[2]. There we need to download the appropriate installer for the operating system the user is using and running it on the machine. This is the best way to get Python in Windows machines.

- MacOS comes with Python already installed, but typically it is an older version (namely, 2.x.x). The best way to install Python then is through an amazing open source package manager called Homebrew[3]. The installation of Homebrew is very simple and takes just one single command from a terminal. One the package manager is installed, you can select additional libraries and make them available for the whole system[4]. For instance, installing Python requires a simple:

```
brew install python3
```

- Linux systems come with *package managers* which allow to select single libraries to install. There are plenty of managers and they

---

[1]Even if Python is already available in the system, it can be outdated or you might just want to customize the original installation. It is perfectly fine to overwrite the original software.

[2]https://www.python.org/downloads/.

[3]https://brew.sh.

[4]Homebrew is a powerful tool for MacOS. It can be used to manage almost any library or package which comes from Linux world. If you are a Mac user, we strongly encourage you to check it out.

are strictly related to the type of distribution is in use. The most common ones are *yum* (for Red-Hat[5] or Fedora[6]-like systems), *dpkg* and *apt* (for Debian[7]-like systems)[8].

- A final method to install everything you need to start working with Python is through a suite called Anaconda[9]. The main advantage of such thing is that it automatically installs several tools so you don't have to worry to get them later on. To give you an example, below you find an image of the Anaconda Navigator interface which shows all the available software.

---

[5]https://www.redhat.com/en.

[6]https://getfedora.org.

[7]https://www.debian.org/index.html.

[8]The main difference between *dpkg* and *apt* is that the former is not able to manage software dependencies. Moreover, *apt* successfully exploits multiple sources to get the requested packages.

[9]https://www.anaconda.com.

FIGURE 1.2: Anaconda Navigator interface (source: Anaconda, Inc. 2018).

1.7   How Do You Interact with Python?

In one way or another, we were able to install everything and now we are ready to start coding in Python. Now let's be fair: Python on its own is really ugly. It is just an empty and sad window with almost no colors which seems to be very unfriendly to newcomers. If you do not believe us, take a look below.

```
[[franz@rancor] franz2 (:|✔)> python3
Python 3.6.5 (default, Jun 17 2018, 12:13:06)
[GCC 4.2.1 Compatible Apple LLVM 9.1.0 (clang-902.0.39.2)] on darwin
Type "help", "copyright", "credits" or "license" for more information.
[>>> print('Hello World')
Hello World
>>> █
```

FIGURE 1.3: The raw Python terminal interface.

One of the most important things to do when starting to work with a programming language is to choose an effective way to interact with the code. In other words, we want to have a graphical interface which makes it easier to write the code, to spot mistakes, to debug the code, and more broadly to talk with Python. As you can imagine, there exist plenty of graphical interfaces. We refer to these software as *Integrated Development Environment*(s) or IDE(s). In the following lines, we offer a brief tour through the most common and the most effective IDEs you can use.

1.7.1 Spyder

Spyder[10] is for sure one of the most famous IDEs which has been around for a while. It is directly available with Anaconda and you can lunch it by opening Anaconda Navigator. Below you can find the typical interface that Spyder offers.

As you can see, in just a single window you are informed about the folders tree (left panel), the Python code you are writing (center panel) and the different objects you have created during the current session (top-right panel). Also, in the bottom-right panel you have immediate access to the Python console which is exactly the one shown in Figure 1.3.

A very handy characteristic of Spyder is the ability to execute a single line of Python code. This enables very precise control of the flow when developing a code and it is also useful when in the process of spotting mistakes and errors. Since it comes with Anaconda, Spyder is a multi-platform software.

1.7.2 Jupyter Notebook

Jupyter Notebook[11] (commonly just called Notebook) is an open-source web-based application which makes your browser of choice the

---

[10]https://www.spyder-ide.org.
[11]https://jupyter.org.

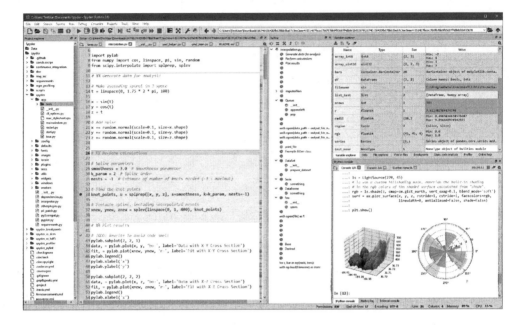

FIGURE 1.4: The Spyder interface (source: The Spyder Website Contributors).

perfect IDE in which develop all your Python codes. Notebook is a lightweight environment and it is extremely portable. It can contain live code, equations, visualizations as well as descriptive text.

Jupyter Notebook also requires a bit of knowledge in a typesetting language called *Markdown*. A good starting point to grasp this language is Markdown Guide[12]. This is a very powerful tool to draft the documentation accompanying the code.

The Notebook interface is pretty simple and neat. When you lunch it, it opens up a new tab in a browser window where you can immediately start writing your Python code. This is one of the best and fastest tool to start developing code. If you want to start using it, we also recommend the so called *Notebook Extensions*. There are different ways you can use go with to install these extensions. The Jupyter Contributions[13] is a very

---

[12]https://www.markdownguide.org.

[13]https://jupyter-contrib-nbextensions.readthedocs.io/en/latest/install.html.

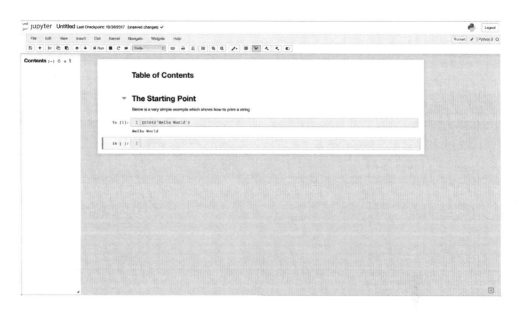

FIGURE 1.5: The Jupyter Notebook interface.

good place to learn how to add them to your default installation.

1.7.3   PyCharm

PyCharm[14] is one of the most powerful and complete IDEs available. It comes in two versions: the Community Edition (CE) and the Professional Edition. The former is available for free and offers fewer features, the latter comes with a commercial licence. For most users, the CE is the way to go, especially when one is starting his/her journey into the world of programming languages.

As you can see, you have all the information needed to develop the code. It includes a very helpful auto completion system and a debugging tool to spot bugs and errors. PyCharm is definitely the tool to use once the code is in its final version and can be widely used and adopted both in a research environment, but also within a business unit in a firm.

---

[14]https://www.jetbrains.com/pycharm/.

FIGURE 1.6: The PyCharm CE interface.

1.7.4   An outsider: iPython

Remember the first picture of a Python terminal shown in Figure 1.3? Well, there is a slightly better version which is just a bit more informative than the standard terminal. It is called iPython[15] and basically can be use for very quick deployment or just testing. Personally, we use it to check that modules have been installed correctly.

As you can see, iPython enhances the standard terminal. For instance, we do have syntax highlighting here as well as the exact number of code executions we run.

---

[15]https://ipython.org.

```
[[franz@rancor] franz2 (:|✔)> ipython3
Python 3.6.5 (default, Jun 17 2018, 12:13:06)
Type 'copyright', 'credits' or 'license' for more information
IPython 7.1.1 -- An enhanced Interactive Python. Type '?' for help.

[In [1]: print('Hello World')
Hello World

In [2]: ▮
```

FIGURE 1.7: The iPython terminal.

Chapter 2

First Steps With Python

2.1 The Logic Behind A Code

Programming is the process of telling a computer what to do. Learning that language allows us to write a set of instructions and rules, potentially very complex, which we call **algorithms**. Algorithms are procedures, namely detailed descriptions of how to do something. Think of algorithms as recipes that tell a computer how to perform a given task.

A very good question to start with is: what is the typical structure of a recipe? Well, we can think of several different ways to structure a recipe but in the world of programming languages, let's consider two main sections:

1. the ingredient part, where we detail all the ingredients that we need to gather to prepare a dish;
2. the instruction part, where we detail how these different ingredients need to be combined, the actions that we need to perform to prepare the dish, and the order in which these actions need to be combined.

Codes (or scripts, or more in general algorithms) are very similar to a recipe. They consist of objects (i.e., basic ingredients) and statements (i.e. instructions about how to combine these objects).

2.2 Objects in Python

If you remember the brief description we provided in Section 1.3, we should know that everything in Python can be considered as an *object*. Objects are entities which we can create, interact with, manipulate and so on. There are plenty of objects that we can create in Python. An object in Python is just an abstraction for data and has three very important characteristics:

1. **Identity.** Once you create an object, its identity does not change.

2. **Type.** It determines the type of operations that we can perform with an object. For instance, you can take the average of a string. As the identity, type cannot be changed unless you force a change.

3. **Value.** It is the content of the object. Think of on object as a little box which the computer stores at a specific memory location. The value is what we store in that box and because of the dynamic semantics, the value of a given objects can be changed.

Let us add another very important concept which is *mutability*. One of the first distinctions that Python considers, regards the mutability of a defined object. If the value of an object can be modified after its definition, then we refer to it as a *mutable* object. Conversely, if no changes are allowed, then we refer to *immutable* object. Consider the following example in which we have a `list` and a `tuple`. Let's ignore for now what these objects are but just focus on their mutability skills.

```
my_list = [1, 2, 3]
my_tuple = (1, 2, 3)
print(my_list, my_tuple)
## [1, 2, 3] (1, 2, 3)
my_list[0] = 10
```

```
print(my_list)
## [10, 2, 3]
```

As you can see, we have been able to modify the first element of the object `my_list` from the value 1 to the value 10. Now let's try to do the very same operation on the tuple `my_tuple`.

```
my_tuple[0] = 10
## TypeError: 'tuple' object does not support item assignment
```

In this case, we simply get an error. This is, in practice, the difference between mutable and immutable objects. There are several types of objects and we will explore the most important ones in the following sections.

Creating objects in Python is really easy. You just have to think about a good naming scheme (we can talk about naming convention if you want) and then you use the assignment operator =. For instance, we just want to create an object that contain the year when mankind fist landed on the Moon. Here is what you need to do:

```
landed = 1969
```

This sounds silly but still, how do we change the value of a variable? Well, we just use assignment operator =. Below is a simple example of multiple changes in the value of a variable. This is pure dynamic semantics at work.

```
test_variable = 1
print(test_variable)
## 1
test_variable = 3.14
print(test_variable)
## 3.14
```

```
test_variable = 'Hello World!'
print(test_variable)
## Hello World!
```

2.3 Object Types

As in the real world, objects can be of different types. Intuitively, an object containing the value 1969 is very different from an object containing the value Houston, we have a problem. We always need to be aware of the type of the objects we are dealing with since this allows certain operations and forbids others. So for instance, we cannot calculate the average of Houston, we have a problem.

In the following sub-sections we will introduce the reader to the most common types which are part of the daily life of a programmer.

2.3.1 Integers

Integers are the simplest objects and are the most efficient ones since they consume the least amount of memory. Integers are either positive or negative numbers with no decimal digits. The mathematical symbol to identify the set of all the integer numbers is $\mathbb{Z}$. Of course, since they are numbers we are allowed to carry out mathematical operations.

So let's define an integer landed by using the assignment operator =.

```
landed = 1969
```

Now, we know that this is an integer just because we defined it this way. But, how do we know if an object is an integer? More in general, how do we know the type of a given object? Well, we ask Python to show us the type by using the command type(). The way we do this is to explicitly ask Python to print the type as follows:

```
print(type(landed))
## <class 'int'>
```

As we can see, we are returned with the information `'int'` which is the Python way to say integer. Everything else is the way Python reports this information which is always the same: `<class 'type of class'>`. Another important aspect is that we used two functions: `type()` and `print()`. Functions play a major role in Python and we will learn how to use them later on in the book. Functions are always applied by invoking them using their name together with parenthesis: `my_function()`.

We learned how to get information about the type. What if we want to print the value contained in the object `landed`? Well, this is very simple: we just use `print()` together with the object as follows:

```
print(landed)
## 1969
```

2.3.1.1 Basic Operations with Integers

Just remember: integers are number so you are good to go to carry out arithmetical operations on them. All we have to do is to provide instructions to Python through *statements*. So let's suppose we want to know how many years have passed since the first manned Moon landing. For instance, we can defined another integer storing the current year, `this_year`, and then subtract the year of landing.

```
this_year = 2018
print(this_year - landed)
## 49
```

If we care about storing that information, we can simply store the value into a new variable. Since the new variable, `delta_t`, is the result of a simple subtraction between two integers, it will be an integer as well.

```
delta_t = this_year - landed
print(delta_t)
## 49
print(type(delta_t))
## <class 'int'>
```

We can do lots of operations with integers. All we need to know is what operation we want to do and the corresponding Python operator. Below is a list of the most common mathematical operations as well as the related operator:

- Addition: +
- Subtraction: -
- Multiplication: *
- Division: /
- Power: **
- Modulo: %
- Integer division: //.

2.3.2   Floats

We are very happy with integers as long as we do not have to deal with decimals. For instance, is the number 3.14 an integer? Let's see:

```
pi = 3.14
print(type(pi))
## <class 'float'>
```

Well, it seems we have to deal with another type of number: the *float*. A float is basically a decimal number and belongs to the set of real numbers $\mathbb{R}$. It can be the results of a division for instance.

```
floating = 2 / 5
print(floating)
## 0.4
print(type(floating))
## <class 'float'>
```

Now, let's complicate things a little bit more. Suppose we have a floating number like our beautiful `floating` variable we just defined. What if we want to force it to be an integer? Well, we can cast the result as integer with the method `int()`. We need to be aware though that Python rounds the result to the lower integer. This is not the regular rule when approximating decimal points. See the example:

```
floating_now_integer = int(2 / 5)
print(floating_now_integer)
## 0
type(floating_now_integer)
## <class 'int'>
floating_now_integer = int(4 / 5)
print(floating_now_integer)
## 0
type(floating_now_integer)
## <class 'int'>
```

2.3.3 Strings

Do you remember when we first started this Section? We said that the objects 1969 and `Houston, we have a problem` were very different. We just learned that the number 1969 is an integer, so what is the second object? It is called *string* and is the opposite type of an integer or a float number. Intuitively, a string is a contiguous set of *characters* in between *quotation marks*. More precisely, the user can specify a string object by using both double " and single ' quotation marks. As we will see below, this textbook adopts both styles since in Python, we can either have single and double quotation marks. So remember: *everything that is in between quotation marks can't be a number.*

The very first we learn from strings is that we are not allowed to take any arithmetical operations on them. Let's to back to the Moon and define our first string:

```
problem = 'Houston, we have a problem.'
print(type(problem))
## <class 'str'>
```

We notice how the type has now changed to `str`. One of the most particular yet counter intuitive features of strings is that they can be number too. Without adding confusion here, what we mean is that we can define the year 1969 as a string. All we have to do is to surround it with quotation marks.

```
landed_string = '1969'
this_year_string = '2018'
print(type(landed_string), type(this_year_string))
## <class 'str'> <class 'str'>
```

If they are strings as we just confirmed, this implies that we cannot do any operation, like the subtraction we did before.

```
this_year_string - landed_string
## TypeError: unsupported operand type(s) for -: 'str' and 'str'
```

As we can see, Python complains that it does not have the correct operator so it does not know what to do with the above statement.

One question could then be: what kind of operations can we actually carry out on strings? We can for example count how many characters a string contains. To do this, we the method `len()` as follows:

```
print(problem)
## Houston, we have a problem.
n_char = len(problem)
print(n_char)
## 27
```

If you go ahead and try to count the characters you will notice that they are not 26. This is because `len()` counts every kind of characters including spaces and punctuation. In the string `problem`, we have 3 spaces and 1 comma which contribute to the total length of the string to get the exact value of 27.

2.3.3.1 Basic Operations with Strings

Let's define a new string as follows:

```
again = 'This is Houston, say again please.'
```

Now suppose that we want to concatenate the string `problem` with the string `again`. How should we proceed? There are different ways in which we can achieve our goal and the simplest one is with the operator +. This is quite counter intuitive since we are accustomed to think that a + just does the sum between two or more numbers. It turns out that we can apply the addition operator to strings and the result is a concatenation of those strings. So let's concatenate `problem` with `again` and define a new string call `communication`.

```
communication = problem + '\n' + again
print(communication)
## Houston, we have a problem.
## This is Houston, say again please.
```

Well, this is not very elegant since we have a very long string which does not fit in the page and we do not know who is talking. What we can do, is manually add other strings to `communication` as follows:

```
communication = 'Apollo 13: ' + problem + '\n' + \
                'Base Houston: ' + again
print(communication)
## Apollo 13: Houston, we have a problem.
## Base Houston: This is Houston, say again please.
```

As we can see, we now have a more readable output. There are two things that happened in the above code chunk. The first one is the command \n which tells Python to insert a newline. The second one is the isolated backslash \ at the end of the first line. This is a handy shortcut to tell Python that the current instruction will be over multiple lines.

2.3.3.2 Concatenate Strings and Numbers

We just learned how to concatenate two string. Now this seems very fancy, but the real magic is when you can actually mix numbers and strings. So let's define some other variables to play with.

```
callsign = 13 # this is an integer
houston = 'you are go for transposition and docking.'
apollo = 'Roger that, Houston.'
```

The goal here is to define the variable `communication` with the following structure: *"13, you are go for transposition and docking. - Roger that, Houston."* The spirit of this operation is very similar to what we did in the previous sub-section. So, let's try to replicate everything as follows:

```
communication = callsign + ' ' + houston + ' - \n' + apollo
## TypeError: unsupported operand type(s) for +:'int'and'str'
```

Ehm....what's wrong? What did we miss? Python is complaining because it is not able to mix integers and strings. Look at the error that Python is throwing:

```
TypeError: unsupported operand type(s) for +: 'int' and 'str'
```

So how do we solve it? Well, remember that we can change types, right? This is exactly what we should do right now. All we want to have is the object `callsign` to be a string and not an integer. To achieve this, we have two ways: the former is a permanent conversion, the latter is just a temporary one. In this last case, we understand that `callsign` is the number 13 and we want to preserve the type. We want to change it on-the-fly and just for this example. We then use the method `str()` directly when defining `communication` as follows:

```
communication = str(callsign) + ', ' + houston + \
                ' - \n' + apollo
print(communication)
## 13, you are go for transposition and docking. -
## Roger that, Houston.
```

Even if it does not make much sense, we can convert `callsign` to string in a permanent way by redefining the variable. Of course, we do not include `str()` during the subsequent concatenation of the strings.

```
callsign = str(callsign)
communication = callsign + ', ' + houston + \
                ' - \n' + apollo
print(communication)
## 13, you are go for transposition and docking. -
## Roger that, Houston.
```

As you can see, the final result is exactly the same.

2.3.4   Formal String-Number Concatenation

What we have just seen is a quick way to concatenate strings and numbers. There is indeed a formal method to concatenate these types of objects. The syntax is less intuitive, but we strongly encourage you to use this last method which is way more handy and flexible than the first one.

The trick is the usage of *placeholders*. Placeholders are just mute variables that assume a specific value once we invoke the method. For the specific case of string-number concatenation, we use the method `format()`.

In order to show and understand the working principle, let's just replicate what we just did, but with this new method. But first, remember that we permanently changed `callsign` to string. To illustrate this method, we want to cast it back to an integer. So, here is the tricky syntax:

```
callsign = 13 # recasting to integer
communication = '{0}, {1} - \n{2}'.format(callsign,
                                           houston,
                                           apollo)
print(communication)
## 13, you are go for transposition and docking. -
## Roger that, Houston.
```

As you can see, many things happened! To learn how to apply this method, just try to follow these five steps:

1. First define the structure of your output. In our case we want something like:

   `string comma space string space dash space newline string`

2. Once you have the structure, you use the placeholders with the syntax `{0}`, where the sequence must start with 0 since Python counts from zero. You put a placeholder instead of the real variable, whether it is a string or a number. Your structure then becomes:

   `{0} comma space {1} space dash space newline {2}`

3. Append the command .format(). The dot (.) is the Python way to dispatch methods on a specific object type. In this simple case, the object is the string structure we are creating.

4. Make sure you respect the order of the structure in .format(). In our example, we first want callsign, then a comma, then the variable houston, then a space a dash a space and a newline and then the variable apollo. Placeholders {0}, {1}, and {2} are references to the three defined objects callsign, houston, and apollo, respectively. The command then becomes:

   ```
   {0} comma space {1} space dash space newline {2}
   .format(callsign, houston, apollo)
   ```

5. Just replace spaces, punctuation, newlines and whatever else with real characters to obtain the final results as follows:

   ```
   {0} , {1} - \n {2} .format(callsign, houston, apollo)
   ```

This seems very complex at first and the untrained reader could ask: what is the advantage of this method? This is a perfectly legit question so let us answer as follow: you can forget about types! As you can see, by no meaning we had to force callsign to a string with str() or in the permanent way. In other words, .format() handles types automatically which comes really handy when we need to structure complex concatenations.

2.3.5 Boolean

Outside a computer, life is much easier in some ways. You just have numbers and strings. In a computer though, we can have things which are neither numbers nor strings. An example is the type called *boolean*. A boolean is basically a flag which tells you either True or False.

Why do we care about this? Well, being able to check that something is true or false is very important. For instance, a boolean is what Python returns if you ask it things like 2 > 1 or 1 > 2. This in the end means to compare two objects.

```
print(2 > 1)
## True
print(1 > 2)
## False
```

If we want, we can define booleans pretty easily as follows:

```
a_true  = True
a_false = False
output = 'a_true is a {0}. \na_false is a {1}.' \
        .format(type(a_true), type(a_false))
print(output)
## a_true is a <class 'bool'>.
## a_false is a <class 'bool'>.
```

This is just a little preview on this very particular type of object. It will return widely when we will talk about conditional statements.

2.4   Commenting the Code

What if we do not want to re-run our script from the beginning? What if we want to insert in the code descriptions and explanations of what we are doing? Right now, this seems a minor problem as it takes a few seconds to re-run it. However, when we will have long scripts, with complex statements, re-running the script from the beginning may be a serious drawback as it will take a lot of time to do it.

Since we do not want to waste our time, a quick solution is to comment out that part of script we are not interested in any longer. There are two ways to achieve that:

1. Comment out a line: You can simply insert the hashtag symbol #
   at the beginning of the line you do not want to run.

2. If we want to comment out an entire block of code we can insert
   triple quotation marks ''' before and after the block we want to
   comment out. Even this might be useful, we strongly recommend
   to insert single line comments only

Let's see this with an example to illustrate how to comment out one
single line. We do not want to print the value of the variable b.

```
a = 1
print(a)
## 1
b = 2
# print(b)
```

Let's see this with an example[1] to illustrate how to comment out a
block of code. We do not want to define the variable b and to print its
value.

```
a = 1
print(a)

'''
b = 2
print(b)
'''
```

---

[1]The fact that the statement `print(a)` is not executed is due to issues of the
interpreter to correctly understand multi-line comments. Again, try to avoid the use
of this method to comment out the code.

2.5   Reserved Keywords

You should have noted that some words get highlighted. Syntax highlighting plays a major role in code development since it helps and guides the programmer when drafting the code. If a word is highlighted, it means that the word has a specific intended behavior in Python. There exist several different keywords which are *reserved keywords*. This implies that you are not allowed to use these keywords other than for their intended goal. For instance, you cannot assign a variable with the name `print`. Other examples of reserved keywords are:

> `and`, `break`, `continue`, `else`, `elif`, `except`, `for`, `if`, `import`, `in`, `is`, `list`, `not`, `or`, `pass`, `return`, `try`, `while`.

We will learn the meaning of these keywords later on in the book.

2.6   Exercises

Exercise 1

1. Create a string `mood` that contains the description of your mood, and a string `program` that contains the name of the program that you are learning right now.

2. Print the message: `'I am <MOOD> to learn <PROGRAM>'` using both the simple `+` operator and the `.format()` method.

Exercise 2

1. Define an integer called `number` and assign it the value 5

2. Print the message: `'Python is the <NUMBER>th program that I learn'`

3. If you feel very *pythonian*, you can modify the message to comply with first, second and third place.

Exercise 3

1. Define a string variable `course` and an integer variable `grade` and give them some values of your choice.
2. Print the message: `'My favorite class was <COURSE> because I got <GRADE>'`, by formatting the string to use your values.

Exercise 4

1. Print: `'I will be 100 years old in the year <x>'`

Please do not create a variable `year` with the year in which you will be 100 years old, but find a way to let Python calculate this year.

2.7   Read the Code

What are the results of the following codes?
Reading 1

```
var1 = 5
var2 = 45
var3 = 10
print((var1 + var2) / float(var3))
```

Reading 2

```
var1 = 5
var2 = 45
var3 = 2.2
print(( var1 + var2) / var3)
```

Reading 3

```
brand = "Coca Cola"
competitor = "Pepsi"
print('I prefer {0} over {1}'.format(brand, competitor))
```

2.8   Code Bloopers

Please fix the errors in the following code.

Blooper 1

```
name = "Ryan"
age  = 19
food = "cheese"

print(name + " is " + age + "\n." \
      "His favorite food is " + food)
## TypeError: must be str, not int
```

2.9   Solutions to Exercises

Exercise 1

```
mood    = 'happy'
program = 'Python'

print('I am ' + mood + ' to learn ' + program)
## I am happy to learn Python
print('I am {0} to learn {1}'.format(mood, program))
## I am happy to learn Python
```

Exercise 2

```
number = 5
print(program + ' is the ' + str(number) + \
      'th program that I learn')
## Python is the 5th program that I learn
out = '{0} is the {1}th program that I learn'.format(program,
                                                     number)
print(out)
## Python is the 5th program that I learn
```

Exercise 3

```
course = "Marketing"
grade  = 30
print('My favorite course was ' + course + \
      '. I got ' + str(grade))
## My favorite course was Marketing. I got 30
print('My favorite course was {0}. I got {1}'.format(course,
                                                     grade))
## My favorite course was Marketing. I got 30
```

Exercise 4

Solution 1

From birth to 100 (When was I born? Then add 100).

```
age   = 24
now   = 2018
birth = now - age
print("I will be 100 in the year " + str(birth + 100))


# Alternatively
## I will be 100 in the year 2094
print("I will be 100 in the year " + str(now - age + 100))
## I will be 100 in the year 2094
```

Solution 2

Remaining years (how many years do I still have to live to make it to 100?).

```
remaining = 100 - age
year = remaining + now
print ("I will be 100 in the year "  + str(year))


# Alternatively
## I will be 100 in the year 2094
print ("I will be 100 in the year " + str(100 - age + now))
## I will be 100 in the year 2094
```

Please note that you do not need to create the variable `birth`, but you can just make the calculation within the `print` statement.

Chapter 3

Tuples, Lists, Sets, and Dictionaries

As we might already know, Python is a very handy programming language. This is not to be confused with poverty or with a limited number of features. Python is one of the most flexible and powerful programming language which contains tons of features.

For instance, we have just seen the simplest set of objects that we can play with: integers, floating numbers, strings, and booleans. Python though is packed with several other objects which play a major role in programming. In this chapter, we are going to focus on more complex objects which serve a specific need.

3.1 Tuples

A tuple is a relatively simple object. It is just a sequence of values separated by a comma. One the most important peculiarities of these objects is that they are *immutable*. We have seen a preview of the mutability feature in the previous chapter so we will reprise the concept here.

```
first_tuple = 1, 2, 3, 4, 5
print(first_tuple)
## (1, 2, 3, 4, 5)
```

As you can see, putting commas in between values defines a tuple. Though it is not a requirement, we strongly recommend to use a more formal, and clear, definition as follows:

```
first_tuple = (1, 2, 3, 4, 5)
print(first_tuple)
## (1, 2, 3, 4, 5)
```

The reason is simple: it improves the readability of the code. The minute we see a sequence of values in between parentheses we immediately know that's a tuple. If you want to be sure about the type of the object, you can always invoke the method `type()` which works here too.

```
print(type(first_tuple))
## <class 'tuple'>
```

Sometimes Python can be a bit nasty and we have to be aware when this happens. In particular, we need to pay attention to the syntax. Look at the following example:

```
test1 = ('a')
test2 = ('a',)
```

What is the type of `test1` and `test2`?

```
print(type(test1))
## <class 'str'>
print(type(test2))
## <class 'tuple'>
```

It turns out that to define a tuple with just one element, it does not matter the type of that single element, we must add a comma after that element. If we do not do this, then Python thinks you are just being verbose and assumes the original type of the element you are using. In the case above, `'a'` is a string so `test1` is cast as a string.

3.1.1 Slicing Tuples

Now that we can deal with sequences of elements, one fair question we can ask is: what if we want to extract the value of the n-th element of a tuple? In other words, how do we access to the tuple's elements? Accessing to elements of an object of this type is called *slicing* and Python allows you do to this by using brackets `[]`. In particular, we type brackets right after a tuple name and we put the position of the element we want to extract inside the brackets. Back to our example, `first_tuple`, let's extract element in position 3 which corresponds to the value 3.

```
print(first_tuple)
## (1, 2, 3, 4, 5)
print(first_tuple[3])
## 4
```

Hey, wait a minute! We can count and 4 is not the value we expected. What's wrong here? Just remember, Python starts counting from zero and not one. So if we want the third element in a tuple, we have to access to position 2 as follows:

```
print(first_tuple)
## (1, 2, 3, 4, 5)
print(first_tuple[2])
## 3
```

Extracting single element is just fine, but probably we would be more interested in accessing to a sequence of elements. So for example, what

would we do to extract the first three elements? We introduce here the
colon operator :. This basically tells Python to build a sequence that
starts from the element on the left of : up to the element before the
number on the right of :. In mathematical terms, it means that we have
a closed set on the left and an open set on the right. Extracting the first
three elements implies that we want the elements in position zero, in
position one, and in position two. As you can see below, we have to tell
Python to move up to element in position three which is open and it is
not extracted.

```
print(first_tuple[0:3])
## (1, 2, 3)
```

So more in general, if we want to extract a sequence from element in
position i up to element in position j we have to specify the following
statement: `my_object[i:j+1]`.

As you can imagine, there exist plenty of ways to slice an object.
Below you can find some other examples.

```
# Extracting all the elements
print(first_tuple[0:])
## (1, 2, 3, 4, 5)
```

```
# Extracting the reversed sequence
print(first_tuple[::-1])
## (5, 4, 3, 2, 1)
```

```
# Extracting specific non-contigous indexes
print((first_tuple[0], first_tuple[2]))
## (1, 3)
```

```
# Extracting just the last element
print(first_tuple[-1])
## 5
```

3.1.2   Assigning and Chaining Tuples

Because tuples are immutable objects, we are not allowed to explicitly modify their values. Let's go back to our tuple `first_tuple` and try to change the value of first element 1 with the value 10.

```
first_tuple[0] = 10
## TypeError: 'tuple' object does not support item assignment
```

Any set of multiple objects which is comma-separated is by default cast as tuple. This of course changes if you specify something else (e.g. for instance if you use brackets as for lists).

```
a, b = (1, 2), (3, 4)
print(a)
## (1, 2)
print(b)
## (3, 4)
```

In Table 3.1, we show a quick and concise list of possible operations we can carry out over tuples.

TABLE 3.1: A concise list of possible operations over tuples.

Python Expression	Results	Description
`len((1, 2, 3))`	3	Length
`(1, 2, 3) + (4, 5, 6)`	(1, 2, 3, 4, 5, 6)	Concatenation
`('Hi!',) * 4`	('Hi!', 'Hi!', 'Hi!', 'Hi!')	Repetition
`3 in (1, 2, 3)`	True	Membership
`for x in (1, 2, 3): print x`	1 2 3	Iteration

3.2 Lists

A list is nothing else than another sequence of data. They are definitely the most versatile objects in Python and you are going to use them quite a lot to do all sort of things. You can define a list pretty much the same way you define a tuple, but remember, you need to use brackets []. Another extremely important feature of lists is that they are *mutable* objects. This of course is the opposite of tuples so now we can actually modify the value of a given element in the list. Now let's define our first list:

```
first_list = [1, 2, 3, 4, 5]
print(type(first_list))
## <class 'list'>
print(len(first_list))
## 5
```

In case you are wondering it, list, as well as tuples, support all types meaning:

```
a = ['a', 'b', 'c']
b = [True, False, True]
c = [1, 'a', True]
print(type(a))
## <class 'list'>
print(type(b))
## <class 'list'>
print(type(c))
## <class 'list'>
```

Since they are mutable objects, we are entitle to run more operations on them. Supported operations mimic the ones we have seen for tuples but here we find two interesting methods to modify a list: `append()` and `del`.

3.2.1 Updating a List

Let's suppose that we want to update an existing list meaning that we want to add a value to this list. The method that we have to use is `append()` and it is very intuitive. `append()` always the given value at the end of the list.

The list `a` contains the first three letters of the alphabet. We want to add the fourth one.

```
print(a)
## ['a', 'b', 'c']
a.append('d')
print(a)
## ['a', 'b', 'c', 'd']
```

Beware, that if you keep doing append, you will just add the element you are appending over and over again.

```
a.append('d')
a.append('d')
a.append('d')
a.append('d')
print(a)
## ['a', 'b', 'c', 'd', 'd', 'd', 'd', 'd']
```

As opposed to the simplest way to define a list, we can also use a list of variables to pass to the list. Say for instance that we want to create a list with the members of a very (VERY) famous rock band. Let's do it![1]

```
band1  = ['Paul McCartney', 'George Harrison',
          'John Lennon', 'Ringo Starr']
bass   = 'Paul McCartney'
guitar = 'George Harrison'
singer = 'John Lennon'
drums  = 'Ringo Starr'
band2  = [bass, guitar, singer, drums]
```

```
print(band1)
## ['Paul McCartney', 'George Harrison',
## 'John Lennon', 'Ringo Starr']
print(band2)
## ['Paul McCartney', 'George Harrison',
## 'John Lennon', 'Ringo Starr']
```

Now we can ask Python to check if the two lists are identical.

---

[1]We invite the reader to ignore the for loops here. These are used with the sole aim at making the Python output more readable.

```
print(band1 == band2)
## True
```

3.2.2 Deleting a List Element

So far, we now know how to update a list with the method `append()`. What if we want to delete a specific element? We can use the method `del`. For instance, let's delete one of the member of this very famous band. We want to delete Paul McCartney who is the first element of the list.

```
del band1[0]
print(band1)
## ['George Harrison', 'John Lennon', 'Ringo Starr']
```

3.2.3 Slicing Lists

Intuitively, we would like to apply what we learned for tuples to lists too. We can retrieve a sub-list by defining a range of list indices, separated by the colon operator :. Let's create a list called `list1` which we will slice in different ways.

```
list1 = [3, 5, 7, 9]
```

```
# Slice one element
print(list1[0])
# Slicing a sequence
## 3
print(list1[0:3])
# Slicing up to the last element
## [3, 5, 7]
print(list1[-2:])
# Slicing up to the second element
```

```
## [7, 9]
print(list1[:2])
## [3, 5]
```

A very handy shortcut to extract sub-lists is by *step size*. So far, we have discussed how to slice consecutive elements in a list. But what if we are interested in non-consecutive elements? If these elements are at a regular distance, we can still select them by adding a third parameter inside the slicing operator. This third parameter is called `step size`. Technically, this third parameter is included in any slice operator, but since the default is equal to 1 we typically do not add it when we are interested in consecutive elements. For instance, let us assume that we want to print all the elements in odd positions in `list2` defined as follows:

```
list2 = [1, 2, 3, 4, 5, 6, 7, 8, 9, 10, 11, 12]
```

From the computer perspective, printing all the elements in odd positions means that we want elements at a regular interval of 2. The syntax we use follows this logic: starting point, ending point, step size.

```
print(list2[0:-1:2])
## [1, 3, 5, 7, 9, 11]
```

3.3 Indexing

We have already seen the concept of slicing objects. Slicing allows us to access or extract specific subsets of elements in a given object. Each element has a specific *index* which marks its position in the object. There are many objects that we can slice in particular lists. Lists are particularly helpful in a variety of contexts, which you will appreciate later. Most notable, we will use lists to run iterations and write more efficient algorithms. As you might imagine, lists are flexible and powerful objects which allow us to perform operations faster than with variables. Indexing comes in three ways:

1. *Forward indexing*: from the first element to the last. The first element of a list has always index 0. The second element has then index 1 and so on and so forth.

2. *Negative indexing*: from the last element to the first. The last element of a list has index -1. This indexing is particularly helpful when we do not know how many elements are in the list, but we just know that we want the last one. The second-to-last element has index -2, and so on and so forth.

3. *Mixed indexing*. It is a combination of the former two ways of indexing.

Oh, just a reminder: Python indexes always start at 0 rather than at 1. This is a powerful source of errors! Because of this, when we want to access to the last element we must use -1 and we can't just invoke `len()`. See the example below.

```
test_list = [1, 2, 3, 4, 5]
print(len(test_list))
## 5
```

Now we extract last element which has value 5 and it is at position 4.

```
# The first one assumes you now the exact
# position of the last element
print(test_list[4])
## 5
```

```
# This instead directly looks for the last element
print(test_list[-1])
## 5
```

```
print(test_list[len(test_list)])
## IndexError: list index out of range
```

3.4   Exercises on Lists

Exercise 1

1. Create a list of the Beatles' members and assign it to the variable
   `beatles`.
2. Create the variables `bass`, `guitar1`, `guitar2`, `drummer` that stores
   the names of each Beatles' members. Assign these variables as
   elements of a list `list_beatles`.

Note: you are allowed to google the Beatles if you don't know either
members or instrument. Shame on you!

Exercise 2

Given a list `a = [5, 10, 15, 20, 25]`,

1. create a list `b` that contains only the first and last elements.

Exercise 3

Describe yourself using the following set of lists:

- ["red", "brown", "blond", "black"]
- ["green", "brown", "blue"]
- [50, 55, 60, 65, 70, 75, 80, 85, 90].

Please do the following:

1. Fill in the gaps with your characteristics. *E.g., I have .... hair, ...*
   eyes, and I weight less than... kilos.
2. Be sure to use at least two methods to concatenate strings.

Exercise 4

Given this list b = [3, 5, 8, 13, 2, 4, 50, 23, 53, 9, 11],
create a list c with the following elements: 3, 8, 2, 50, 53.

Exercise 5

1. Create a list with your latest 5 grades so far.
2. Calculate the GPA of your last three exams.

Exercise 6 - Revise your GPA

1. You go to the exam review and discover that your second-to-last
   grade is 24 rather than 27.
2. What is your new GPA of your last three exams?

3.5 Python Methods

A formal definition of method is the following:

A method is a function which belongs to a class.

In other words, methods are specific functions that can be applied to specific objects that we have created. A `method` is a function that is tightly coupled to some objects. Since we still do not know what a function is, this definition will probably sound obscure at this point. So, in plain terms, a method is a *shortcut* to perform an operation on an object.

Since someone has already written the set of commands to perform that operation, we simply *invoke* the method with no need to rewrite the commands behind it. The syntax to call methods is always the same:

```
object.method(arguments)
```

To understand how to apply methods, let's consider the following logical steps:

1. We start with the **name** of the object.

2. A dot . follows the name of the object. This is Python syntax so whenever you see a dot . you know you are calling a method.

3. The **method** followed by parentheses (). If you are wondering why you need parentheses, well...a method is a function.

4. Inside the parentheses, we put the **argument(s)**: namely, specific elements of the object upon which we want to perform the method. Argument(s) can be optional and for some methods they are not required. However, even if we will not pass any argument, we would still need the parentheses. If you don't put (), Python will complain a lot and the command won't be executed.

The syntax we just discussed is general and applies to any Python object. Once again, depending on the object type we can *dispatch* a given set of methods. In the following Section, we go over methods applied over lists.

3.5.1   Methods for Lists

Let us now introduce the most common methods for lists. They are mostly used for fetching, storing, and of course analyzing data.

3.5.1.1   `append()`

We have already seen this method when we were discussing ways to update a list. So once again, `append()` allows you to physically add new information to the current list. Let us go back to our list a:

```
a = ['a', 'b', 'c']
```

We want to add the fourth alphabet letter to a. We use `append()` as follows:

```
a.append('d')
'a after the append method is {0}'.format(a)
## "a after the append method is ['a', 'b', 'c', 'd']"
```

The careful reader could ask the following question: why do not we assign the *updated* list to a new list or just to the same list? The concept around why we do not have to this is fundamental. Python applies the method `append()` *in-place*.

3.5.1.2   `insert()`

`append()` is the way to go if you want...well...append an element at the very end of the list. Now suppose that we are interested in inserting a new information at a specific position which might be in the middle of the list. Well, we have another method called `insert()` which handles this issue.

The syntax is very simple and it's a good example of the usage of function arguments:

```
your_list.insert(index, element)
```

This method takes two arguments:

1. `index`: the index marking the position where we want to insert an element;
2. `element`: the element we want to insert.

Let us suppose that we want to add the integer 15 in position 3 to our original list `firs_list`. We can do it with the following command:

```
print(first_list)
## [1, 2, 3, 4, 5]
first_list.insert(2, 15)
out = "After adding 15 in position 3, \n" \
      "first_list becomes {0} ".format(first_list)
print(out)
## After adding 15 in position 3,
## first_list becomes [1, 2, 15, 3, 4, 5]
```

3.5.1.3 extend()

If instead of just one single element, we want to add several elements to the end of a list, we would use the method `extend()`. For instance, let us assume that we want to add the integers 3, 13, 15, and 17 to the updated `first_list`. First, we create `second_list` that contains the integers we want to add:

```
second_list = [3, 13, 15, 17]
```

We want to extend `first_list` with `second_list` as follows:

```
first_list.extend(second_list)
out = "Updated first_list is {0}".format(first_list)
print(out)
## Updated first_list is [1, 2, 15, 3, 4, 5, 3, 13, 15, 17]
```

3.5.1.4   index()

If we want to know the index of an element in a list we can use the method `index`. It returns the index of the first occurrence of an element in a list. Thus, we can print the index of the element 3 in `first_list` as:

```
out = "The first occurrence of 3 in first_list \n" \
      "has index {0}".format(first_list.index(3))
print(out)
## The first occurrence of 3 in first_list
## has index 3
```

3.5.1.5   count()

This method returns the number of times a certain element occurs in a list. For instance, to print the number of times the element 3 occurs in `list1` we can run the command:

```
print("The integer 3 occurs %d times in list1" \
      %(list1.count(3)))
## The integer 3 occurs 1 times in list1
```

This is probably the most complex command we have written so far. We have learned how to insert the results of a method directly in the `print` statement. However, this time we are adding a further layer of complexity with another *placeholder*: %. You can learn the meaning of a placeholder in the tip box.

TIP: Placeholders

A placeholder is a pre-formatted object into which we can place values. It is indicated with the percentage sign %. What comes after the % indicates the type of the object we will insert in the placeholder:

- %d acts as a placeholder for a number;
- %s acts as a placeholder for a string.

The syntax to replace a placeholder is: %s %d (name, number). Inside the parentheses we insert the value we want to place in the placeholder. When we have multiple placeholders, the value of each placeholder is separated by commas. As usual, respecting the order is important!

QUESTION: can you suggest a case in which we would like to use this approach instead of `format()`?

In Table 3.2, you can find a quick list of methods for lists.

TABLE 3.2: A quick list of methods for lists.

METHOD	OUTCOME	SYNTAX	PARAMETER
Append	Adds an item to the end of a list.The list is updated	`list1.append(item)`	**element**: the element to add (number, string, another list, dictionary, etc.)
Clear	Removes all items from the list.The list is deleted	`list1.clear()`	NONE
Copy	Returns a copy of the list	`list1 = [1, 2, 3] list2 = old_list.` **REMEMBER**: When you modify `list2`, `list1` is automatically modified too!	NONE
Count	Returns the number of occurrences of an element in a list	`list1.count(element)`	**element** - element whose count is to be found.

METHOD	OUTCOME	SYNTAX	PARAMETER
Extend	Extends the list by adding all items of a list (passed as an argument) to the end. The list is updated	`list1.extend(list2)`	It takes a single argument (a list)
Index	Searches an element in a list and returns the index of its first occurrence	`list1.index(element)`	**element**: the element to search.
Insert	Inserts the element to the list at a given index. The list is updated	`list1.insert(index, element)`	**index**: the index of the position where to insert element; **element**: the element to insert
Pop	Removes and returns the element at the given index (passed as an argument) from the list. The list is updated.	`list1.pop(index)`	**Index**: the index of the element to be removed. If no parameter is passed, the default index -1 is passed as an argument
Remove	Searches for an element in a list and removes the first occurrence of that element. The list is updated	`list1.remove(element)`	**element**: the element to remove
Reverse	Reverses the elements of a list.The list is updated	`list.reverse()`	NONE
Sort	Sorts the elements of a list. The list is updated	`list1.sort(reverse=...)`	**reverse** - If true, the sorted list is sorted in descending order

3.5.2   Exercise on Methods

Exercise 1

1. Create a group with you and the person on your right.
2. Now, add the person on your left to the group.

Exercise 2

Add the person in front of you AND the person on your left/right.

3.5.3   The zip() function

We can *zip* together two or more lists to create a list of tuples. The result has the length of the shortest zipped list, other items are ignored:

```
names  = ["Kirs", "Paul", "Mark"]
grades = [29, 30, 22, 25, 26]
```

```
students = zip(names, grades)
print(students)
## <zip object at 0x10fabca08>
print(type(students))
## <class 'zip'>
students_tuple = tuple(students)
print(type(students_tuple))
## <class 'tuple'>
```

Look carefully at your new list. What do you notice?

3.6   Sets

Now we are taking one further step forward in complexity. We have seen tuples and lists and we learned that they are basically sequence of values of either the same type or different one. What we have also seen is that it is perfectly fine to have a list which contains repetitions. Think about grades... it is quite common that more than one student get the same grade so you have, say, 26 repeated for all the students that got 26.

Now were are changing this last behavior. Sets are an *unordered collections* of *unique* elements. Conversely from lists that may contain repeated elements, a set does not allow that. Moreover, they are immutable objects like tuples. We cannot change the elements of a set. So lets' wrap everything up:

> *A set is an immutable and unordered collection of unique elements.*

3.6.1 How to Create a Set

We know that the = is our friend when we need to create an object so we know that we have to use it. But now we also need to explicitly declare the type of object we want to create. Whether with tuples and lists Python provides us with shortcuts like () and [], this is not the case with sets... almost.

We then create a set by calling the function `set()` and applying it to a list as follows:

```
set1 = set([1, 2, 3, 3, 4, 4, 5, 5, 6, 7, 8, 9, 0])
print(set1)
## {0, 1, 2, 3, 4, 5, 6, 7, 8, 9}
```

If you do not want to waste too much time or simply do not want to be too verbose, we can use the following shortcut:

```
set2 = {1, 2, 3, 3, 4, 4, 5, 5, 6, 7, 8, 9, 0}
print(set2)
## {0, 1, 2, 3, 4, 5, 6, 7, 8, 9}
```

```
print(type(set2))
## <class 'set'>
```

Do you see the nice curly braces encapsulating our set? Well, that's your shortcut!

The diligent reader may have noticed a contradiction here: we say that sets are collections of unique elements but then in set1 we have several non-unique elements. Let us see if we really have non-unique elements in set1 by counting how many elements are in it:

```
print(len(set1))
## 10
```

Python returns 10, which is the number of unique elements in set1. Hence, even though we may have non-unique elements in a set, Python always consider each element just once. This property of sets will turn particularly helpful when downloading large amount of data in several batches, so to avoid counting the same element (e.g., a Twitter account's follower) twice. Common uses of sets include membership testing, removing duplicates from a sequence, and standard math operations on sets such as intersection, union, difference, and symmetric difference.

3.6.2 Methods for Sets

As lists, sets too have their own methods that facilitate performing operations with them. We look in detail at two of them, union and intersection. Set methods follow the general syntax for methods so we will invoke them through ..

3.6.2.1 union()

Given two sets, we may be interested in knowing the elements that belong to *both* sets. For instance, let us suppose that we are promoting an event related to soccer in Milan. We have two sets, `milan` and `inter`, which contains the top 3 supporters of each team, respectively. We can create a third set `mail` which is the mailing list of all the supporters of the two teams. Let's do this:

```
milan = set(["Kirs", "Paul", "Frank"])
inter = set(["Javier", "Mauro", "Kirs"])
print("Milan is supported by", milan)
## Milan is supported by {'Kirs', 'Frank', 'Paul'}
print("Inter is supported by", inter)
## Inter is supported by {'Kirs', 'Mauro', 'Javier'}
mail = milan.union(inter)

print("The union of Milan and Inter supporters is\n", mail)
## The union of Milan and Inter supporters is
##  {'Paul', 'Mauro', 'Javier', 'Kirs', 'Frank'}
```

Please note that we can compute the union of more than one set at the same time. For instance, if we had another set `real` that contains the top 2 supporters of Real Madrid, we can compute the **union** of the three sets by adding `real` as a second argument of the method `union()` as follows:

```
real = set(["Jorge", "Sergio"])

print("Milan U Inter U Real is\n", milan.union(real, inter))
## Milan U Inter U Real is
## {'Paul','Jorge','Javier','Mauro',
##  'Kirs','Frank','Sergio'}
```

3.6.2.2 `intersection()`

This method returns the elements that are common to all sets. If we want to know all the supporters in common between Milan and Inter, we type:

```
print("Milan IN Inter is", milan.intersection(inter))
## Milan IN Inter is {'Kirs'}
```

If we want to know all the supporters who root for the three teams, we type:

```
print("Milan IN Inter IN Real is", \
      milan.intersection(inter, real))
## Milan IN Inter IN Real is set()
```

By combining what we have learned so far, can you tell Python to print a sentence like this:

"Milan, Inter, and Real have <x> supporters in common"?

```
print("Milan, Inter, and Real have %d supporters in common" \
      %(len(milan.intersection(inter, real))))
## Milan, Inter, and Real have 0 supporters in common
```

In Table 3.3 you can find a quick list of methods for sets.

TABLE 3.3: A quick list of methods for sets.

METHOD	OUTCOME	SYNTAX	PARAMETER
remove	Searches for the given element in the set and removes it	`set1.remove(element)`	**element**: The element to remove. It takes just one argument
add	Adds a given element to a set. Remember: if the element is already in the set, it doesn't add any element	`set1.add(element)`	**element**: The element to add. It takes just one argument
copy	Returns a copy of the set	`set1 = set([1,2,3])` `set2 = set1` **REMEMBER**: When you modify `list2`, `list1` is automatically modified too!	NONE
clear	Removes all elements from the set	`set.clear()`	NONE
difference	Given two sets, set1 and set2, it returns the set of elements that exists only in `set1` but not in `set2`	`set1.difference(set2)`	**set**: the set to control
discard	Removes a specified element from the set (if present)	`set.discard(element)`	**element** : The element to discard. It takes just one argument
intersection	Returns a new set with elements that are common to all sets	`set1.intersection(set2)`	An arbitrary number of arguments. Each argument is the name of the set to calculate intersection with

METHOD	OUTCOME	SYNTAX	PARAMETER
isdisjoint	Returns True if two sets are disjoint sets (i.e., they have no element in common). If not, it returns False	`set1.isdisjoint(set2)`	**set**: the set to control. It takes just one argument
issubset	Returns True if all elements of a set are present in another set (passed as an argument). If not, it returns False	`set1.issubset(set2)`	**set**: the set to control
pop	Returns an arbitrary (random) element from the set. The set is updated and does not contain the element.	`set.pop()`	NONE
symmetric_difference	Returns a new set which contains the elements that are in either in set1 or in set2 but not in both	`set1.symmetric_difference(set2)`	
union	Returns a new set with distinct elements from all the sets	`set1.union(set2)`	An arbitrary number of arguments. Each argument is the name of the set to calculate union with
update	Adds elements from a set (passed as an argument) to the set	`set1.update(set2)`	**set**: The set to add. It takes a single argument

3.6.3   Exercises on Sets

Exercise 1 - Find the Murderer

Victor Plum was killed in the studio with a knife by one of his heirs! Find the murderer!

1. The following people are Plum's heirs: Diane, Eleanor, Kassandra, Jacob.
2. The following people were in the studio: Eleanor, Jack, Diane.
3. The following people own a knife: Jacob, Diane, Kassandra.

3.7   Dictionaries

It is now the time to add another layer of complexity. All we have seen till now involves sequence of values, whether they are numbers or strings, unique or not, immutable or mutable. In this Section, we want to associate *keys* with all those values. Whenever we have keys, we have a dictionary. In other words, a dictionary associates keys with values. They are named after ordinary paper dictionaries because they work analogously. A `key` (the word you want to look up) is associated with a `value` (the definition of a word). Let's review the definition:

A dictionary associates a unique key with a specific value.

3.7.1   How to Create a Dictionary

Long story short, we define dictionaries using {} or `dict()`. We need to pay attention here since the symbol {} has been already used to define sets. Here we have keys though and this marks the difference between sets and dictionaries. Python uses the same symbol to define both the object types. To associate keys with values we use the colon operator :. Let's define the dictionary `grades` as follows:

```
grades = {"Kirs": 29, "Paul": 30, "Mark": 22}
print(grades)
## {'Kirs': 29, 'Paul': 30, 'Mark': 22}
print(type(grades))
## <class 'dict'>
```

One question we could ask is: what if we want to create an empty dictionary? We simply use {} and as you can see we get a dict type.

```
grades = {}
print(type(grades))
## <class 'dict'>
```

Keys are *unique* within a dictionary while values may not be. The values of a dictionary can be of any type, but the keys must be of an immutable data type such as strings or integers. Keys cannot be lists because they can be changed after their creation. So key duplication is not allowed but let's see what happens when we use the same key twice... here you go!

```
grades = {"Kirs": 29, "Paul": 30, "Mark": 22, "Kirs": 18}
print(grades)
## {'Kirs': 18, 'Paul': 30, 'Mark': 22}
```

As you can see, grades returns the last value associated with the duplicated key which in this case is "Kirs" with value 18.

3.7.2 Casting and Recasting Objects

In this Section, we focus on moving from one object type to another. Let us assume that we have two lists: names and grades which store the names of three students and their grades, respectively. We want to create the dictionary student_grades that has the defines names as keys and grades as values. But first, let's create the two lists:

```
names  = ['Kirs', 'Paul', 'Mark']
grades = [29, 30, 22]
```

If you remember, we have seen a very useful function called `zip()`. This function returns by default a list of tuples. We also know that if we want to change the default type of the object returned by `zip()`, we need to recast it to what we are requiring. In this case, we want to move from a list to a dictionary as follows:

```
student_grades = dict(zip(names, grades))
print(student_grades)
## {'Kirs': 29, 'Paul': 30, 'Mark': 22}
print(type(student_grades))
## <class 'dict'>
```

This is exactly what we wanted to do. To check we are doing everything correctly, let's manually define the dictionary and compare the two. We expect a `True` as output from the last line below:

```
student_grades_manual = {"Kirs": 29, "Paul": 30, "Mark": 22}
print(student_grades == student_grades_manual)
## True
```

Now we start to realize that Python is really smart. We also start to realize why this is a high-level programming language. If we analyze what Python just did, we can appreciate how by just declaring that we wanted a dictionary as outcome, it immediately interpreted the first argument, `names`, as keys and the second argument, `grades`, as values. This is very powerful and it allows us to focus on the manipulation of the data, their analyses and modelling rather than just thinking about the logic behind each instruction.

3.7.3 Retrieving a Value

Accessing a value works similar as indexing in lists, but instead of the index given as an integer number, we use the defined key(s). Of course, we always use the brackets [] as follows: `dictionary_name[key]`. Let us see how to retrieve, for instance, the value (grade) of Paul:

```
print(student_grades["Paul"])
## 30
```

What if the key did not exist?

```
print(student_grades["John"])
## KeyError: 'John'
```

Python complains and informs you the there is a `KeyError`.

3.7.4 Setting Values

Dictionaries are mutable objects so we can add new entry to a dictionary or change an existing one as follows:

```
print(student_grades)
## {'Kirs': 29, 'Paul': 30, 'Mark': 22}
student_grades["Abbie"] = 27 # add a new entry
print(student_grades)
## {'Kirs': 29, 'Paul': 30, 'Mark': 22, 'Abbie': 27}
student_grades["Mark"]  = 27 # change existing entry
print(student_grades)
## {'Kirs': 29, 'Paul': 30, 'Mark': 27, 'Abbie': 27}
```

3.7.5 Multi-level dictionaries

Dictionaries are complex objects, meaning that they can have complex structures. For instance, if the values of a dictionary are dictionaries themselves, we have a *multi-level dictionary*[2].

So let's define a more complex dictionary in which we are interested in both grades and skills of the students. The keys in the first level are the `names` of the students and their associated values are dictionaries with the keys `grades` and `skill`.

```
students = {"Kirs": {"grades": 29, "skill": "Engineering"},
            "Paul": {"grades": 30, "skill": "Math"},
            "Mark": {"grades": 22, "skill": "Latin"}
        }
```

```
print(students)
## {'Kirs': {'grades': 29, 'skill':'Engineering'},
## 'Paul': {'grades': 30, 'skill': 'Math},
## 'Mark': {'grades': 22, 'skill': 'Latin'}}
```

3.7.6   Exercises on Dictionaries

Exercise 1

Refer to the dictionary `students` defined above.

1. Retrieve all the information about Paul.
2. Now, retrieve Paul's skill.

3.8   Solution to Exercises

3.8.1   Solutions to Exercises on Lists

Exercise 1

1. Create a list of the Beatles' members and assign it to the variable `beatles`.

---

[2]A case in which you can find this structure is when we retrieve data from Twitter.

2. Create the variables `bass`, `guitar1`, `guitar2`, `drummer` that stores the names of each Beatles' members. Assign these variables as elements of a list `list_beatles`.

Note: you are allowed to google the Beatles if you don't know either members or instrument. Shame on you!

Solution 1

```
beatles = ["Paul","John", "George", "Ringo"]
print(beatles)
## ['Paul', 'John', 'George', 'Ringo']
```

Solution 2

```
bass = "Paul"
guitar1 = "John"
guitar2 = "George"
drummer = "Ringo"

list_beatles = [bass, guitar1, guitar2, drummer]
print(list_beatles)
## ['Paul', 'John', 'George', 'Ringo']
```

Exercise 2

Given a list a = [5, 10, 15, 20, 25],

1. create a list b that contains only the first and last elements.

```
a = [5, 10, 15, 20, 25]
b = [a[0], a[-1]]
print(b)
## [5, 25]
```

Exercise 3

Describe yourself using the following set of lists:

1. ["red", "brown", "blond", "black"]
2. ["green", "brown", "blue"]
3. [50, 55, 60, 65, 70, 75, 80, 85, 90].

Please do the following:

1. Fill in the gaps with your characteristics. *E.g., I have .... hairs, ... eyes, and I weight less than... kilos.*
2. Be sure to use at least to methods to concatenate strings.

```
hair = ["red", "brown", "blond", "black"]
eyes = ["green", "blue", "brown"]
weights = [50, 55, 60, 65, 70, 75, 80, 85, 90]
```

Solution 1

```
print("I have", hair[-1], "hair,", eyes[1],
      "eyes, and I weight less than",
      weights[-2], "kilos.")
## I have black hair, blue eyes, and I weight less than 85 kilos.
```

Solution 2

```
out = 'I have {0} hair, {1} eyes and I weight less than ' \
      '{2} kilos.'.format(hair[-1],
                          eyes[1],
                          weights[-2])
print(out)
## I have black hair, blue eyes and I weight less than 85 kilos.
```

Solution Exercise 4

Given this list b = [3, 5, 8, 13, 2, 4, 50, 23, 53, 9, 11], create a list c with the following elements: 3, 8, 2, 50, 53.

```
b = [3, 5, 8, 13, 2, 4, 50, 23, 53, 9, 11]
c = b[:-2:2]
print(c)
## [3, 8, 2, 50, 53]
```

Solution Exercise 5

1. Create a list with your latest 5 grades so far.
2. Calculate the GPA of your last three exams.

Solution 1

```
grades = [30, 28, 25, 27, 30]
gpa = (grades[-1] + grades[-2] + grades[-3]) / 3.
print(gpa)
## 27.333333333333332
```

Solution 2

```
grades = [30, 28, 25, 27, 30]
gpa = sum(grades[-3:]) / 3.
print(gpa)
## 27.333333333333332
```

Solution Exercise - Revise your GPA 6

1. You go to the exam review and discover that your second-to-last grade is 24 rather than 27.
2. What is your new GPA of your last three exams?

Solution 1

```
grades[-2] = 24
gpa = sum(grades[-3:]) / 3.
print(gpa)
## 26.333333333333332
```

3.8.2 Solutions to Exercises on Methods

Exercise 1

1. Create a group with you and the person on your right.
2. Now, add the person on your left to the group.

```
group = ["Marco", "Arianna"]
group.append("Frank")
print(group)
## ['Marco', 'Arianna', 'Frank']
```

Exercise 2

1. Now, add the person in front of youAND the person on your best friend.

```
new_members = ["Nico", "Francesco"]
group.extend(new_members)
print(group)
## ['Marco', 'Arianna', 'Frank', 'Nico', 'Francesco']
```

3.8.3 Solutions to Exercises on Sets

Exercise 1 - Find the Murderer

Victor Plum was killed in the studio with a knife by one of his heirs! Find the murderer!

1. The following people are Plum's heirs: Diane, Eleanor, Kassandra, Jacob.
2. The following people were in the studio: Eleanor, Jack, Diane.
3. The following people own a knife: Jacob, Diane, Kassandra.

```
heirs = set(["Diane", "Eleanor", "Kassandra", "Jacob"])
studio = set(["Eleanor", "Jack", "Diane"])
knife = set(["Jacob", "Diane", "Kassandra"])


murderer = heirs.intersection(studio, knife)
print(murderer)
## {'Diane'}
```

3.8.4 Solutions to Exercises on Dictionaries

Exercise 1

Refer to the dictionary students defined above.

1. Let us assume that we want to retrieve all the information about Paul. As we did before, we will use the related key from the higher-level dictionary students as follows

```
print("All we know about Paul is", students["Paul"])
## All we know about Paul is {'grades': 30, 'skill': 'Math'}
```

2. Now, let us assume that we want to retrieve Paul's skill. Inside, the sub-dictionary Paul, we need to add the lower-level key skill as follows:

```
print("Paul's skills is", students["Paul"]["skill"])
## Paul's skills is Math
```

Chapter 4

Conditional Statements and Loops

To understand what a conditional statement does, just think about what an *if* does in real life. For instance, let's suppose that you want to be noticed about how many coffee your coffee shop sold *if* the number of coffee sold is higher than 10. In other words, we want to have something along the following lines:

> *"If we sell more than 10 coffee, just let me know it."*

There may be cases when you need to execute a block of code several times in a row. When this is the case, conditional statements are not enough. We need to use slightly more complex structures called *loops*. Loops are literally everywhere, so it is fundamental to understand how they work.

In this chapter, we discuss two very common, but important loops:

1. `for` loops;
2. `while` loops.

So let's try to built a simple code that mimics the sentence above. In order to be able to use conditional statements correctly, we must add one more very important concept called *indentation*.

4.1   Indentation

If you remember, last time we discussed an unusual Python characteristic: the complete absence of parentheses which delimit a given block of instructions. We also discussed that most of the programming languages use curly braces {} to address this specif issue. So the question is: how do we define a block of instructions in Python?

The magic concept which comes in handy here is called *indentation*. Python understands that if a given instruction is indented with respect to the previous one, this implies that it belongs to a separated block of instructions. In general, a new block starts right after a special command which is represented by colons :[1]. Usually, most IDEs will help you in getting the right indentation. Where it is manually needed, just remember that the correct indentation is given by pressing the `TAB` key once, or by putting four consecutive spaces.

4.2   if Statements

To visualize the statement, let's take a look at Figure 4.1 which depicts the logic behind an `if`-statement.

Going back to our coffee, let's pretend that using `print()` will do the job of signaling the number of coffee sold. We just need to put the *if* in place so that Python understands when to invoke the `print()`. The syntax for `if` statements is very simple: you just need to use the reserved keyword `if`.

---

[1] We have seen colon operator when we were slicing tuples and lists. The use here is very different.

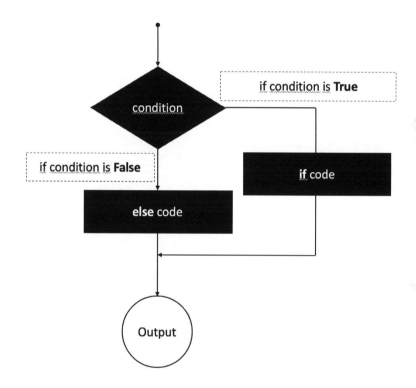

FIGURE 4.1: The Conceptualization of if-statement.

Let's do this:

```
n_coffee = 5
if n_coffee >= 10:
  print('You just sold more than 10 coffee')
```

Please note here the indentation after the `if` statement. As you can see, Python didn't print anything since we have sold just 5 coffee. Below, we sold 20 so the condition in the `if` is true so Python correctly prints the message.

```
n_coffee = 20
if n_coffee >= 10:
    print('You just sold more than 10 coffee')
## You just sold more than 10 coffee
```

As you can imagine, there are several ways to use `if` statements meaning that you can have different condition controls. In Table 4.1 you can find a quick list of the most common operators.

TABLE 4.1: A quick list conditional operators.

Expression	Mathematical Symbol	Python Expression
Less than	$<$	<
Greater than	$>$	>
Less than or equal	$\leq$	<=
Greater than or equal	$\geq$	>=
Equals	$=$	==
Not equal	$\neq$	!=

Also, in Table 4.2, we can compare objects in the following way:

TABLE 4.2: A quick list of types of object comparisons.

Expression	Python Expression
x and y are the same object	x is y
x and y are different objects	x is not y
x is a member of y	x in y
x is not a member of y	x not in y

In case you want to concatenate multiple conditions, you can use the additional commands **and** and **or**. For instance, you can request to being informed if you sold between 10 and 20 coffees as follows:

```
n_coffee = 19
if n_coffee >= 10 and n_coffee <= 20:
    print('You just sold between 10 and 20 coffees')
## You just sold between 10 and 20 coffees
```

Alternatively, you always have an **or** condition which gives you just two different option. For instance, you just want to know if you sell less than 10 coffee or more than 20 as follows:

```
n_coffee = 2
if n_coffee <= 10 or n_coffee >= 20:
    print('You just sold less than 10 or ' \
          'more than 20 coffees')
## You just sold less than 10 or more than 20 coffees
```

4.3   else Statements

If statements can solve several problems. One question you can ask though is: how can we have a way out? Meaning, how can we code something like:

> *"If we sell more than 10 coffee, just let me know it otherwise apply a 10% discount."*

The word *otherwise* is translated in Python by the reserved keyword `else`. and the use is similar to `if`. Of course, there wouldn't be any otherwise without an `if` so the `else` command works in conjunction with `if`. Let's write in Python the above statement:

```
n_coffee = 5
if n_coffee >= 10:
    print('You just sold more than 10 coffees')
else:
    print('Buy a coffee with 10% discount!')
## Buy a coffee with 10% discount!
```

As you can see, Python checked the first condition given by the `if` and found it to be false. Then it checked the way out given by the `else` and found it to be true so it printed the message.

4.4   `elif` Statements

Now let's add one more step. How can we code something like:

> *"If we sell more than 10 coffee, just let me know it but if we sell more than 20 then we offer an orange juice for free. Ah yes, if we sell less than 10 coffee then apply a 10% discount"*

Multiple options in Python are managed by `elif`. As `else` this works only when `if` is already in place.

```
n_coffee = 124
if n_coffee >= 10:
    print('You just sold more than 10 coffees')
```

```
elif n_coffee >= 20:
    print('Here is your free orange juice for you!')
else:
    print('Buy a coffee with 10% discount!')
## You just sold more than 10 coffees
```

Hey, what's wrong here? Why the code doesn't enter in the `elif` block? Well, 20 is always `>=` than 10, so the first condition will always be true. We need to fine tune the first `if` and put an upper bound as follows:

```
n_coffee = 124
if n_coffee >= 10 and n_coffee < 20:
    print('You just sold more than 10 coffees')
elif n_coffee >= 20:
    print('Here is your free orange juice for you!')
else:
    print('Buy a coffee with 10% discount!')
## Here is your free orange juice for you!
```

4.4.1 Condition Check

Whenever we want to use `if` and `elif`, we need to remember that Python enters in the subsequent block of instructions if and only if the condition is satisfied. In other words, if the condition that the statement is checking is found true. This is why whenever we do comparison with the list of operators in the table above, we get a boolean as a response.

4.5 The for Loop

A loop is a mechanism for which computer repeats the same block of codes multiple times. We depict the logic behind a `for` loop in Figure 4.2.

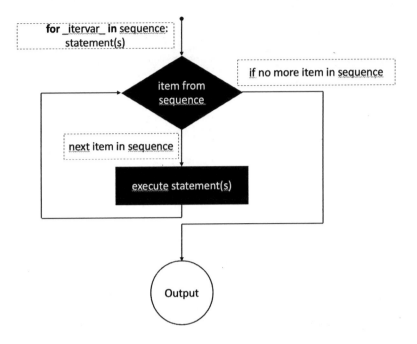

FIGURE 4.2: The Conceptualization of the for Loop

Let's assume that we want to print each element contained in a given sequence of numbers. Our sequence goes from 1 to 5. How can we get Python to print all elements? Well, we can do it manually by remembering that Python, as well as other programming languages, executes the instructions sequentially. So the code at line $n - 1$ will always come before the code at line n.

```
my_sequence = (1, 2, 3, 4, 5)
print(my_sequence[0])
## 1
print(my_sequence[1])
## 2
print(my_sequence[2])
## 3
print(my_sequence[3])
```

```
## 4
print(my_sequence[4])
## 5
```

You immediately realize how simple is to write a loop. But what if the sequence was made by 10^4 elements? Well, we can use the `for` function to make Python automatically scroll through each element of the sequence so that we could execute a given instruction step by step. Let's print all the elements of `my_sequence` with the help of `for`:

```
my_sequence = (1, 2, 3, 4, 5)

for ith_element in my_sequence:
    print(ith_element)
## 1
## 2
## 3
## 4
## 5
```

As you can see, several things happened. Let's proceed with order:

1. the syntax of a `for` loop is as follows:

```
for <element> in <iterable>:
    <instructions>
```

2. `for` and `in` are reserved keywords. One the structure of the loop has been defined, just remember to use the operator : at the end of the line and to indent with a `TAB` or 4 spaces in the new line;

3. `<element>` is a mute variable which only exists within the `for` loop. In the example above, `ith_element` corresponds to the physical values in `my_sequence`;

4. `<iterable>` is the object which we want to scroll. An *iterable* is a collection of elements which can be either fully determined like for tuples, lists, sets, and dictionaries, or a conceptual *iterator* like a range of numbers. We will see that a `for` loop only works with iterable objects;

5. `<instructions>` represents the block of instructions which will be executed in the `for` loop;

6. it's less verbose than before;

7. we don't have to pay attention at specifying the element we want to access;

8. we are getting direct access to the elements of `my_sequence`.

4.5.1   For Loops On Determined Iterables

We anticipated the concept of fully determined iterables and now it is time to explore what this means. Whenever you have a tuple, a list or a dictionary, we can run the `for` loop directly on those objects, which are fully determined.

We need to pay lot of attention on the type of iterable we are dealing with since each has its own different behavior. In order to better understand the concept, take a look at the following examples.

4.5.1.1   `for` Loops Over Tuples and Lists

Looping over these objects has the same effect that we have already seen. Let's create a tuple and a list both containing a sequence from 1 to 5 and print each element

```
my_tuple = (1, 2, 3, 4, 5)
my_list  = [1, 2, 3, 4, 5]
my_list.append(6)


# Loop over a tuple
for _i in my_tuple:
    print(_i)
## 1
## 2
## 3
## 4
## 5
```

```
# Loop over a list
for _j in my_list:
    print(_j)
## 1
## 2
## 3
## 4
## 5
## 6
```

We can also try to print both sequences using just one loop. In this case, the two sequences must have the same length

```
print('Both Sequences')
## Both Sequences
for _i in my_tuple, my_list:
    print(_i)
## (1, 2, 3, 4, 5)
## [1, 2, 3, 4, 5, 6]
```

As you probably noted, `<element>` is a given name with the prefix `'_'`. This is a convention we use a lot to explicitly and visually state which is the mute variable that we are using within the loop.

In Python there is a handy way to access both to indexes and values when looping over an object by using the function `enumerate()`. This takes an iterable object and as `<element>`, you can specify both the index position and the related value as follows:

```
for _i, _val in enumerate(my_list):
    print(_i, _val)
## 0 1
## 1 2
## 2 3
## 3 4
## 4 5
## 5 6
```

As you can see, `_i` represents the indexes, while `_val` represents the values at a specific index.

4.5.1.2   `for` Loops Over Strings

What happens when we have a string and we use a `for` loop over it? Well, you need to think the string as a sequence of elements given by characters. The `for` loop will scroll over them as follows:

```
my_string = ['Hello World']

for _i in my_string:
    print(_i)
## Hello World
```

4.5.1.3 `for` Loops Over Dictionaries

We should remember that a dictionary is a sequence of pairs given by the `key` and its `value`. When we loop over dictionaries, we use just the keys and not the values. Let's loop over the dictionary representing the Beatles.

```python
beatles = {'bass': 'Paul McCartney',
           'guitar': 'George Harrison',
           'singer': 'John Lennon',
           'drummer': 'Ringo Starr'}

for _i in beatles:
    # print the key
    print(_i)
    # print the value at that key
    print(beatles[_i])
## bass
## Paul McCartney
## guitar
## George Harrison
## singer
## John Lennon
## drummer
## Ringo Starr
```

We can print dictionary values by slicing the dictionary using its keys.

```python
for _i in beatles:
    print('Key {0} with value {1}'.format(_i, beatles[_i]))
## Key bass with value Paul McCartney
## Key guitar with value George Harrison
## Key singer with value John Lennon
## Key drummer with value Ringo Starr
```

4.5.2   `for` Loops Over Iterators

What if we wanted a `for` loop over an iterable without directly accessing its elements. In other words, we want to scroll the iterable through its indexes. What makes the job here is `range()` applied over the whole length of the iterable as follows:

```python
my_list = [1, 2, 3, 4, 5]

print(range(len(my_list)))
## range(0, 5)
print(len(range(len(my_list))))
## 5
print(type(range(len(my_list))))
## <class 'range'>
```

```python
for _i in range(len(my_list)):
    temp = _i + 1
    print(temp/5)
## 0.2
## 0.4
## 0.6
## 0.8
## 1.0
```

4.5.3   Creating Lists Through `for` Loops

What if we want to create a new list that stores the results of each iteration (rather than printing it)? You should remember a very important method for lists called `append()`. This what we are about to apply.

Let's create a list with some numbers in it. We want to create a two more lists which contain the squared values and the square root of the elements of the first list.

```
my_list = [2, 4, 12, 15, 25]
my_list_squared = []
my_list_sqrt = []

for _i in my_list:
    temp = _i**2
    my_list_squared.append(temp)
print(my_list_squared)
## [4, 16, 144, 225, 625]
```

Or. . .

```
for _i in range(len(my_list)):
    temp = my_list[_i]**(1/2)
    temp = round(temp, 2)
    my_list_sqrt.append(temp)
print(my_list_sqrt)
## [1.41, 2.0, 3.46, 3.87, 5.0]
```

4.5.4   Iteration Over Multiple Lists

The goal here is to iterate over two lists at the same time. Let's create a list with the first names of some soccer players and a second list with their last names. We want to print their full names.

```
first_names = ["Franco", "Marco", "Paolo", "Pippo"]
last_names  = ["Baresi", "Van Basten", "Maldini", "Inzaghi"]

for _i in range(len(first_names)):
    print(first_names[_i], last_names[_i])
## Franco Baresi
## Marco Van Basten
```

```
## Paolo Maldini
## Pippo Inzaghi
```

Please note that this kind of iteration works just with `for` loops over iterators.

4.5.5   Exercises on `for` Loops Over Lists

Exercise 1
You are the instructor in a class with 5 students.

1. Create the list `grade1` that contains the grades of the mid-term exam (you are allowed to choose 5 different grades by yourself).
2. Curve the grades by adding to 2 points to each grade.
3. Print each grade through an iterable.
4. Print each grade through an iterator.

Exercise 2
Consider the example above about AC Milan players.

1. Define the new list `legends` which contains the full names.
2. Print the new list.

Exercise 3

You have the Beatles in your classroom. This is awesome, but you also get the chance to know their grades: 30, 28, 25, 18.

1. Please create a new list `beatles_grades` with their names, last names, and grades.
2. Print the new list.

E.g., Paul McCartney: 30; George Harrison: 28. . .

```
name    = ["Paul", "George", "John", "Ringo"]
surname = ["McCartney", "Harrison", "Lennon", "Starr"]
grades  = [30, 28, 25, 18]


beatles_grades = []
```

Exercise 4

1. Print a list with the `names` of your best friends, one with their `gifts`, and one with `costs`.

The final result should read: *I will give **name** a **gift**. It costs **price**.*

```
name  = ["Paul", "Kirsten", "David", "Debbie"]
gifts = ["watch", "smartphone", "kindle", "book"]
price = [100, 300, 100, 30]
christmas_list = []
```

4.5.6   `for` Loops Over Dictionaries: Details

We have already seen the behavior of a `for` loop over a dictionary. You basically scroll over keys and not values, at least directly. We have also seen that in order to access a dictionary's value we need to use `[]` and slice the dictionary itself. Let's now assume that we want to print the following sentence:

KEY's grade is VALUE

So let's create a one-level dictionary in which we have 4 students with their grades and we store them in `student_grades`.

```
student_grades = {'Kirs': 29,
                  'Paul': 30,
                  'Mark': 22,
                  'Abbie': 27}
print(student_grades)
## {'Kirs': 29, 'Paul': 30, 'Mark': 22, 'Abbie': 27}
```

We need to remember that a dictionary is an iterable. For this reason, we can use a specific method called `items()`. Because the dictionary comes with two iterable objects in it, KEYS and VALUES all we have to do is to specify two elements as follows:

```
for _key, _value in student_grades.items():
    print(_key, _value)
## Kirs 29
## Paul 30
## Mark 22
## Abbie 27
```

The behavior is pretty similar to the one of `enumerate()`. We have to mute variables, `_key` and `_value`, which represent KEYS and VALUES, respectively. Of course, we can achieve the same result by simply looping over the KEYS and slicing the dictionary. The choice of method depends on the task you are trying to solve.

```
for _i in student_grades:
    print(_i, student_grades[_i])
## Kirs 29
```

```
## Paul 30
## Mark 22
## Abbie 27
```

Even more, we can print more meaningful statements by concatenating strings in the usual way:

```
for _key, _value in student_grades.items():
    print('{0}\'s grade is {1}'.format(_key, _value))
## Kirs's grade is 29
## Paul's grade is 30
## Mark's grade is 22
## Abbie's grade is 27
```

Please note that since we want to explicitly print the symbol ', a quotation mark, we need to escape it using a backslash \. This is mandatory otherwise Python would treat the quotation mark as if we were defining a string so as a formal quotation mark.

4.5.7   for Loops With Multi-Level Dictionaries

So far, we have already seen what a *one-level* dictionary is: you have a key paired with one value. Now, let us assume that we have the dictionary students and we want to print the skills associated with each student. In the language of dictionaries, this means that we have the first level key which indicates the name of the student. The value associated with this key is another dictionary which contains both the grades and the skills. students is defined as follows:

```
students = {"Kirs": {"grade": 29, "skill": "engineering"},
            "Paul": {"grade": 30, "skill": "math"},
            "Mark": {"grade": 22, "skill": "Latin"}
          }
```

Now let's iterate over keys and values of this dictionary.

```
for _key, _value in students.items():
    print(_key, _value)
## Kirs {'grade': 29, 'skill': 'engineering'}
## Paul {'grade': 30, 'skill': 'math'}
## Mark {'grade': 22, 'skill': 'Latin'}
```

We immediately notice that we have three sub-dictionaries, one for each student. Inside this `for` loop, each sub-dictionary is indicated with the key `_key`. Each sub-dictionary `_key` has two more sub-keys: `grade` and `skill`. This time, we are interested in retrieving the values associated to the sub-key `skill`. We know from previous sections that the syntax to retrieve this value is `_key['skill']` so we just plug this inside the `for` loop as follows:

```
for _key, _value in students.items():
    print('{0}\'s best skill is ' \
          '{1}'.format(_key, students[_key]['skill']))
## Kirs's best skill is engineering
## Paul's best skill is math
## Mark's best skill is Latin
```

4.5.8   Exercises on `for` Loops Over Dictionaries

Exercise 1
Consider the dictionary `students`.

1. Print the following statement:

STUDENT got GRADE and the best skill is SKILL.
E.g., Kirs got 29 and best skill is engineering.

4.6   while Loops

We have just learned a way to sequentially execute certain operations. What if instead of following a sequence, we want to repeat a block of instructions? The method that addresses this is issue is called `while`. The rational under the `while` loop is very simple and we depict the logic behind it in Figure 4.3. In words, the concept of this loop goes as follows:

> *While this condition is true, keep executing the following block of instructions. As soon as the condition is not met anymore, so it is false, do something else.*

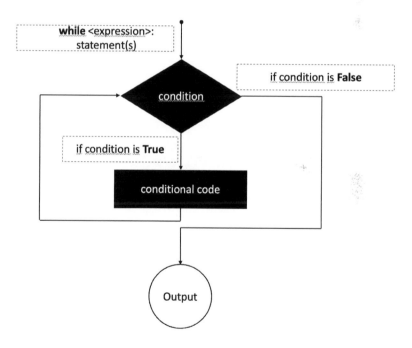

FIGURE 4.3: The Conceptualization of While Loop.

The indented body of the `while` loop repeats *as long as* the predicate following the keyword is true:

```
while <pred>:
    <instructions>
```

Let's see an example of a `while` loop. The following call is executed till the length of the input list is > 0. So as soon as there are no more elements in the list, the `while` loop is terminated. Also, we get to know a new method for lists which is called `pop()`. `pop()` deletes and returns the last element of a list.

```
beatles = ['Ringo', 'John', 'George', 'Paul']
while len(beatles) > 0:
    beatles_popped = beatles.pop()
    print(beatles_popped + ' left the Beatles')
    print('There are {0} Beatles left'.format(len(beatles)))
## Paul left the Beatles
## There are 3 Beatles left
## George left the Beatles
## There are 2 Beatles left
## John left the Beatles
## There are 1 Beatles left
## Ringo left the Beatles
## There are 0 Beatles left
```

As you can see, this entails that something has to happen in the loop in order to change the condition! This is one possible way to terminate a `while` loop. Another way is the following. Let's consider the idea of just printing natural numbers till a given upper bound.

```
count = 0
while (count < 11):
    print('The count is: {0}'.format(count))
    count += 1
## The count is: 0
## The count is: 1
## The count is: 2
## The count is: 3
## The count is: 4
## The count is: 5
## The count is: 6
## The count is: 7
## The count is: 8
## The count is: 9
## The count is: 10
```

As you can see, we define an initial counter called count set to zero. The condition says that we print till count = 10. At the end of each iteration we increment the value of count by 1 using the operator +=.

4.6.1   Exercises on while Loops

Exercise 1

Calculate the square of each number from 1 to 10.

4.7 List Comprehension

Creating list in Python is very easy... but it can pretty quickly turn into something tiresome. For instance, typing in all the values separately can take quite some time and you can easily make mistakes. We are lucky enough though since Python comes with a handy tool called *list comprehension*. This offers you a way to mimic the mathematical notation and to translate it into Python's instructions.

In order to explain what we mean, let's consider the sets, tuples, and vectors which are all mathematical objects. Through the mathematical notation, we can describe these objects as follows:

$$S = \{x^2 : x \text{ in } \{0, \ldots, 9\}\},$$
$$V = \left(1, 2, 4, 8, \ldots, 2^{12}\right),$$
$$M = \{x \,|\, x \text{ in } S \text{ and } x \text{ even}\}.$$

We read these objects as follows:

1. The sequence S is actually a sequence that contains values between 0 and 9 included that are raised to the power of two.

2. The sequence V, on the other hand, contains the value 2 that is raised to a certain power. For the first element in the sequence, this is 0, for the second this is 1, and so on, until you reach 12.

3. Lastly, the sequence M contains elements from the sequence S, but only the even ones.

A bit hard to digest, right? In Python we would do the following:

```
S = [0, 1, 4, 9, 16, 25, 36, 49, 64, 81]
V = [1, 2, 4, 8, 16, 32, 64, 128, 256, 512, 1024, 2048, 4096]
M = [0, 4, 16, 36, 64]
```

So let's build the three lists using the list comprehension way as follows:

```
S = [x**2 for x in range(10)]
V = [2**i for i in range(13)]
M = [x for x in S if x % 2 == 0]

print(S)
## [0, 1, 4, 9, 16, 25, 36, 49, 64, 81]
print(V)
## [1, 2, 4, 8, 16, 32, 64, 128, 256, 512, 1024, 2048, 4096]
print(M)
## [0, 4, 16, 36, 64]
```

It worked! What the code is actually telling you is the following:

1. The list S is built up with the square brackets that you read above in the first section. In those brackets, you see that there is an element x, which is raised to the power of 10. Now, you just need to know for how many values (and which values!) you need to raise to the power of 2. This is determined in range(10). Considering all of this, you can derive that you'll raise all numbers, going from 0 to 9, to the power of 2.

2. The list V contains the base value 2, which is raised to a certain power. Just like before, now you need to know which power, i, is exactly going to be used to do this. You see that i in this case is part of range(13), which means that you start from 0 and go until 12. All of this means that your list is going to have 13 values - those values will be 2 raised to the power 0, 1, 2,... all the way up to 12.

3. Lastly, the list M contains elements that are part of S if-and-only-if they can be divided by 2 without having any leftovers. The modulo needs to be 0. In other words, the list M is built up with the equal values that are stored in list S.

We have just learned `for` loops and as you can see this is a keyword that's coming back in list comprehension. Also, the keyword `in` plays a major role here since this reflects its mathematical formulation. To conclude, the general syntax of a list comprehension is as follows:

```
my_list = [x for x in <iterable>]
```

Or in other words:

```
[<expression> for <item> in <list>]
```

4.8   An Alternative to `for` Loops

The main purpose of a `for` loops is to repeat a block of code a fixed number of times. List comprehensions are actually good alternatives to `for` loops, as they are more compact and directly reflect a mathematical formulation.

Consider the following example that starts with the variable `numbers`, defined as a range from 0 up until 10 (not included). The trick here is that the number you pass to `range()` is actually the number of integers you want to generate. And remember, the sequence starts from zero. Let's try it:

```
n_elements = 20
numbers = range(n_elements)
print(numbers)
## range(0, 20)
```

Let's pretend we want to generate a new list called `new_list` which contains the square of just the even numbers. Let's use a `for` loop here since we know how to do it.

```
# Initialize `new_list`
new_list = []


# Add values to `new_list`
for n in numbers:
    if n%2 == 0:
        new_list.append(n**2)

# Print `new_list`
print(new_list)
## [0, 4, 16, 36, 64, 100, 144, 196, 256, 324]
```

Well, as expected we now master the `for` loops and the conditional statements and we achieved the intended result. Now let's try to do the same task but with list comprehension. We can clearly see the neater and more compact notation.

```
# Create `new_list`
new_list = [n**2 for n in numbers if n%2 == 0]

# Print `new_list`
print(new_list)
## [0, 4, 16, 36, 64, 100, 144, 196, 256, 324]
```

Let's consider another example around sets. Let A and B be two sets, the cross product (or Cartesian product) of A and B, written $A \times B$, is the set of all pairs wherein the first element is a member of the set A and the second element is a member of the set B. Mathematically we have:

$$A \times B = (a, b) : a \text{ belongs to } A, b \text{ belongs to } B.$$

```
colors = [ "red", "green", "yellow", "blue" ]
things = [ "house", "car", "tree" ]

colored_things = [(a, b) for a in colors for b in things]

# we use a for loop to print because
# of printing layout
for _i in colored_things:
    print(_i)
## ('red', 'house')
## ('red', 'car')
## ('red', 'tree')
## ('green', 'house')
## ('green', 'car')
## ('green', 'tree')
## ('yellow', 'house')
## ('yellow', 'car')
## ('yellow', 'tree')
## ('blue', 'house')
## ('blue', 'car')
## ('blue', 'tree')
```

Let's now consider a final example in which we put `if-else` statements as well.

```
obj = ["Even" if i%2 == 0 else "Odd" for i in range(10)]

for _i in obj:
    print(_i)
## Even
## Odd
## Even
## Odd
```

```
## Even
## Odd
## Even
## Odd
## Even
## Odd
```

4.9   Read the Code

Reading 1

```
list1 = [3, 5, 7, 8, 10]
for element in list1:
    element1 = element + 1
    print(element1)
```

Reading 2

```
list1 = [3, 5, 7, 8, 10]
for element in list1:
    element1 = element + 1
print(element1)
```

Reading 3

```
brand     = ["CocaCola", "Pepsi", "MountainDew"]
account   = ["@CocaCola", "@pepsi", "@MountainDew"]
followers = [300000, 200000, 45000]


for _i in range(len(brand)):
    print('The Twitter account of {0} is {1} and has {2}' \
          'followers.'.format(brand[_i],
```

```
                          account[_i],
                          followers[_i]))
```

4.10   Solutions to Exercises

4.10.1   Solutions to Exercises on for Loops Over Lists

Exercise 1

You are the instructor in a class with 5 students.

1. Create the list grade1 that contains the grades of the mid-term exam (you are allowed to choose 5 different grades by yourself).
2. Curve the grades by adding to 2 points to each grade.
3. Print each grade through an iterable.
4. Print each grade through an iterator.

Solution 1

```
grade1 = [23, 25, 28, 26, 30]

for _g in grade1:
    print(_g + 2)
## 25
## 27
## 30
## 28
## 32
```

Solution 2

```
for _g in range(len(grade1)):
    print(grade1[_g] + 2)
## 25
## 27
## 30
## 28
## 32
```

Exercise 2

Consider the example above about AC Milan players.

1. Define the new list `legends` which contains the full names.
2. Print the new list.

```
first_names = ["Franco", "Marco", "Paolo", "Pippo"]
last_names  = ["Baresi", "Van Basten", "Maldini", "Inzaghi"]
legends=[]

for _i in range(len(first_names)):
    temp = first_names[_i] + ' ' + last_names[_i]
    legends.append(temp)

for _i in legends:
    print(_i)
## Franco Baresi
## Marco Van Basten
## Paolo Maldini
## Pippo Inzaghi
```

Exercise 3

You have the Beatles in your classroom. This is awesome, but you also get the chance to know their grades: 30, 28, 25, 18.

1. Please create a new list `beatles_grades` with their names, last names, and grades.
2. Print the new list.

E.g., Paul McCartney: 30; George Harrison: 28...

```
name    = ["Paul", "George", "John", "Ringo"]
surname = ["McCartney", "Harrison", "Lennon", "Starr"]
grades  = [30, 28, 25, 18]


beatles_grades = []
```

Solution 1

```
for _i in range(len(name)):
    beatles_grades.append(name[_i] + " " + surname[_i] + \
                        ": " + str(grades[_i]))
for _i in beatles_grades:
    print(_i)
## Paul McCartney: 30
## George Harrison: 28
## John Lennon: 25
## Ringo Starr: 18
```

Solution 2

```
beatles_grades = []
for _i in range(len(name)):
    beatles_grades.append('{0} {1}: {2}'.format(name[_i],
                                                surname[_i],
                                                grades[_i]))
for _i in beatles_grades:
    print(_i)
## Paul McCartney: 30
## George Harrison: 28
## John Lennon: 25
## Ringo Starr: 18
```

Exercise 3

1. Print a list with the **names** of your best friends, one with their **gifts**, and one with **costs**.

The final result should read: *I will give **name** a **gift**. It costs **price**.*

```
name  = ["Paul", "Kirsten", "David", "Debbie"]
gifts = ["watch", "smartphone", "kindle", "book"]
price = [100, 300, 100, 30]
christmas_list = []
```

Solution 1

```
for _i in range(len(name)):
    complete = "I will give " + name[_i] + " a " + \
               gifts[_i] + ". It costs " + str(price[_i])
    christmas_list.append(complete)
for _i in christmas_list:
    print(_i)
## I will give Paul a watch. It costs 100
## I will give Kirsten a smartphone. It costs 300
## I will give David a kindle. It costs 100
## I will give Debbie a book. It costs 30
```

Solution 2

```
for _i in range(len(name)):
    complete = 'I will give {0} a {1}. ' \
               'It costs {2}'.format(name[_i],
                                     gifts[_i],
                                     price[_i])
    christmas_list.append(complete)
for _i in christmas_list:
    print(_i)
## I will give Paul a watch. It costs 100
## I will give Kirsten a smartphone. It costs 300
## I will give David a kindle. It costs 100
## I will give Debbie a book. It costs 30
## I will give Paul a watch. It costs 100
## I will give Kirsten a smartphone. It costs 300
## I will give David a kindle. It costs 100
## I will give Debbie a book. It costs 30
```

4.10.2   Solutions to Exercises on `for` Loops Over Dictionaries

Exercise 1

Consider the dictionary `students`.

1. Print the following statement:

STUDENT got GRADE and the best skill is SKILL.
E.g., Kirs got 29 and best skill is engineering.

```python
for _key, _value in students.items():
    print('{0} got {1} and the best skill ' \
          'is {2}'.format(_key,
                          students[_key]['grade'],
                          students[_key]['skill']))
## Kirs got 29 and the best skill is engineering
## Paul got 30 and the best skill is math
## Mark got 22 and the best skill is Latin
```

4.10.3   Solutions to Exercises on `while` Loops

Exercise 1

Calculate the square of each number from 1 to 10.

```python
count = 1
while (count < 11):
    print(count**2)
    count +=1
## 1
## 4
## 9
## 16
```

```
## 25
## 36
## 49
## 64
## 81
## 100
print("Done! :-)")
## Done! :-)
```

Chapter 5

Functions

One of the most important thing to remember when coding is the ability to not just save the code, but also reuse it. Python is a functional programming language in the sense that it's been conceived to work with functions.

A function is a block of reusable code that is used to perform a single action. The term function is borrowed from the math. You pass an input to a "mathematical" function and you get an output. Pretty much like mathematical functions, we can use a Python function over and over again and we can expect that its behavior doesn't change with time.

When we want to use a function, we say we *call* or *invoke* the function. Functions are everywhere in Python and we have already seen few of them which are built-in like `print()`, `len()`, `type()`. As you can imagine, we can create our own functions which satisfy our needs. These functions are called *user-defined functions*.

Functions in Python have two main core elements:

1. **header**: the characteristics that defines the function:

    1. the reserved keyword `def` to start declaring the function;
    2. the function name, followed by parentheses `()` (remember, it's a function) and a colon `:`;

3. Inside () you can include optional parameters which are named entities that specify an argument that the function can accept;

2. **body**: all the indented code we write after the definition line:

1. any instruction the function executes;
2. the reserved keyword `return`. The return statement passes a value out of the function. It also stops Python from running the rest of the code in the function. In other words, `return` is the last instruction executed by the function.

The general function syntax looks like this:

```
def <name>(<arguments>):
    <statements>
    return <value>
```

To call a function, we use its name, followed by the parentheses. We have seen this with the built-in function `len()`. As with built-in functions, inside the parentheses, we pass the target object upon which the function will be applied.

5.1   Writing a Function in Python

Let us assume that we want to create a function called `pow2()` that multiplies any number by 2 and `return` the result. We can define the function as following:

```
def pow2(n):
    a = n*2
    return a
```

n is a parameter of the function. In order to get the function to work, we need to specify a value.

Please note how the set of instructions is indented. The final command is `return` which signals the end of the function. After `return`, no more lines of code are executed. The object a exists in the function's scope only. For instance, if we want to call a outside the function, unless we already defined somewhere before in the code, Python will complain that a does not exist. We can apply our function `pow2()` simply as follows:

```
out = pow2(n = 10)
print(out)
## 20
```

We can also chain the outcome of our function with other operations. For example, here we are summing 100 and 10.

```
out = pow2(10) + 10
print(out)
## 30
```

5.1.1 Default Parameters

The function that we just created takes one single parameter and returns a single value. What if we do not pass a value to the function? Let's try it:

```
pow2()
## TypeError: pow2() missing 1 required positional argument: 'n'
```

As you can see, Python complains because it expects an argument. Of course, we can solve this problem by defining a default parameter. For instance, in the absence of a specification, the argument is zero.

```
def pow2(n = 0):
    a = n**2
    return a
```

```
out = pow2()
print(out)
## 0
```

5.1.2   Functions With 2 Arguments

Now, let us assume that we want to create a function `mult()` that takes two numbers and returns the result of their multiplication. Multiple parameters functions can be defined in the same exact way as single parameter ones. We just need to separate arguments with a comma as follows:

```
def mult(arg1 = 0, arg2 = 0):
    a = arg1 * arg2
    return a
```

Now we pass 3 and 4 as parameters and we print the result.

```
out = mult(arg1 = 3, arg2 = 4)
print(out)
## 12
```

5.1.3   The Parameter *args

The question we have in mind when writing this paragraph is: what are all the possible use cases of the function we are writing? The short answer is: we have no idea. What we would like to have though is options. We want to have the most flexible code and we would like to interact with it in the easiest and most general way possible.

For instance, it could be that a user would like to give to our function a variable number of parameters. In Python, the single-asterisk form of `*args` can be used as a parameter to send a *non-keyworded variable-length* argument list to functions. What is really important here is just the asterisk `*` since the name `arg` is there by convention, so you are allowed to choose your favorite one.

Let's go back to our two-parameters function `mult()`. What if we pass three parameters?

```
mult(3, 4, 5)
# Simplify error output
## TypeError: mult() takes 2 positional arguments
## but 3 were given
```

Well, Python is very clear: there is an unexpected keyword since `mult()` only takes two parameters but we are passing three. Let's update the definition of the function by introducing `*args` as follows:

```
def mult(*args):
    a = 1
    for num in args:
        a *= num
    return a
```

Now we apply this updated version using a variable set of parameters:

```
out1 = mult(3, 4)
out2 = mult(3, 4, 5)
out3 = mult(2, 5, 10)
out4 = mult(12, 3, 2, 4)

print(out1, out2, out3, out4)
## 12 60 100 288
```

Using *args to send a variable-length argument list to our function, enable to pass in as many arguments as we wish into the function call. This makes the code way more flexible and even more readable.

5.1.4 The Parameter **kwargs

We can pass even more complicated arguments to a function by using the double asterisk form of **kwargs. This allows us to pass in a *keyworded variable-length argument dictionary* to a function. Again, the important element here is **, as the word kwargs is conventionally used. We adopt this convention to signal that this is a keyworded argument in the form of a dictionary. Similar to *args, **kwargs can take as many arguments as we want. However, **kwargs differs from *args because we have to assign keywords.

To make it simple and easy to follow, let's start by defining a function which print it's own arguments using **kwargs as follows:

```
def func_kwargs(**kwargs):
    print(kwargs)
    return
```

The first thing that we note is that we can actually access to the object which defines the parameters names kwargs (without the double asterisks). The second thing we note is even if the instruction is just a simple print, we use the **return** command anyway with no additional argument. We encourage to always include a **return** at the end of a custom function, especially in the beginning phases of your learning process. Let's pass some arguments then and see what happens[1]:

---

[1]Depending on which Python version you are using, the order of the parameters might change. From version 3.6 on, we have a sorted dictionary based on the order in which we passed the parameters in the function.

```
func_kwargs(first = 'Richard', last = 'Feynman', grade = 30)
## {'first': 'Richard', 'last': 'Feynman', 'grade': 30}
```

As you can see, the parameters are organized in a dictionary in which the keys are given by the parameter names (i.e. first, last, grade) and the values are given by the parameter values (i.e. 'Richard', 'Feynman', 30). What is important now is that we can manipulate this dictionary in the same exact way we did when we first introduced this object type. This is a formal dictionary so it inherits all the related methods. So for instance we can loop over the parameters as follows:

```
def func_kwargs(**kwargs):
    for _key, _value in kwargs.items():
        out = 'The key is {0}, ' \
                'the value is {1}'.format(_key, _value)
        print(out)
    return
```

```
func_kwargs(first = 'Richard', last = 'Feynman', grade = 30)
## The key is first, the value is Richard
## The key is last, the value is Feynman
## The key is grade, the value is 30
```

5.1.5 Formal Order of Parameters

There is a formal order we have to respect when working in combination of positional, keyword arguments and the two special arguments *args and **kwargs. The order is the following:

1. formal positional arguments (i.e. arg1 etc.);
2. *args;
3. keyword arguments (i.e. dictionaries);

4. **kwargs.

So, when working with formal positional arguments like `arg1` and `arg2` in the function `mult()`, the order is as follows:

```
def custom_func(arg1, arg2, *args, **kwargs):
    # some amazing instructions
```

When working with positional parameters along with named keyword parameters in addition to *args and **kwargs, the custom function would look like this:

```
def custom_func(arg_1, arg_2, *args,
           kw_1 = 'hello', kw_2 = 'world', **kwargs):
    # some amazing instructions
```

In conclusion, whenever we are not sure about the number of arguments a function can accept or just receive, we can use the special syntax of *args for standard positional arguments and **kwargs for dictionary-like arguments. We define these in the same way as standard parameters.

As a general advice, we recommend using this approach when you are creating functions that accept a limited number of inputs within the argument list. The primary use of both *args and **kwargs is to increase the readability and convenience of the code. Use them with care since these methods can be tricky.

5.2   Functions Calling Functions

Python is a functional language which means that it is really handy to define custom functions which can be used broadly. One of the possible use could involve the call of a function inside another function.

In order to show the concept, we want to apply the already defined functions `pow2()` and `mult()` one into another one. The idea is to pass two parameters to `mult()` to get their multiplication elevate to the power of two the result. Below, we show again the definitions of the functions and the definition of the new nested function called `mult_pow2()`.

```
def pow2(n):
    a = n**2
    return a
def mult(arg1, arg2):
    a = arg1 * arg2
    return a
def mult_pow2(arg1 = 0, arg2 = 0, n = 0):
    multiplication = mult(arg1, arg2)
    out = pow2(multiplication)
    return out
```

Let's apply this new function as follows:

```
out = mult_pow2(2, 3)
print(out)
## 36
```

As you can see, the function computes the multiplication between 2 and 3 which gives 6, and then computes its second power which leads to 36.

5.2.1   Logical Flow of the Problem

We have just seen a very simple example. Let's assume you want to calculate your final grade, which depends on:

- mid-term grade (30%);
- final exam grade (60%);
- class participation (10%);

As usual, before rushing to Python, it is important to decompose the problem into logical steps. Only after the whole procedure is clear, we will be able to write a Python code to compute our final grade. The problem can be split into sub-problems as follows:

1. calculate the grade of the mid-term exam as: *mid-term * percentage mid-term*;

2. calculate the grade of the final exam as: *final * percentage final*;

3. calculate the class participation grade as: *participation * percentage participation*;

4. sum all the grades.

We are now ready to translate the human logic into a Python code. We will first define three functions that compute the mid-term grade, final exam grade, and class participation grade, respectively. Then, we will define a final function `grade()` that calls these three functions and returns the final grade.

```python
def midterm(mgrade, mperct):
    midg = mgrade * mperct
    return midg
def finalterm(fgrade, fperct):
    finalg = fgrade * fperct
    return finalg
def participation(pgrade, pperct):
    particip = pgrade * pperct
    return particip
def grade(mgrade, mperct, fgrade, fperct, pgrade, pperct):
    out = midterm(mgrade, mperct) + \
            finalterm(fgrade, fperct) + \
            participation(pgrade, pperct)
    return out
```

```
print(grade(28, 0.3, 27, 0.6, 30, 0.1))
## 27.6
```

5.3   Exercises on Functions

Exercise 1
Create a function **square** that calculates the square of 5, 8, and 9
*HINT: You take the power of a number with the ** operator.*

Exercise 2
Create a function **power** that compute the p power of a number.
Then call this function to calculate:

- 5 to the power of 3;
- 8 to the power of 4;
- 9 to the power of 2.

Exercise 3
Please calculate the cost of your Easter vacation by using the following
inputs:

1. The trip lasts 4 nights and 5 days;
2. A night in the hotel costs $100;
3. The airplane ticket costs $300;
4. Renting a car costs $50 per day, and you will need a car for 5 days;
5. Each breakfast will cost $5 (5 breakfasts);
6. Each lunch will cost $20 (5 lunches);
7. Each dinner will cost $45 (5 dinners).

How much will you spend?

5.4   Read the Code

Reading 1

```
def guess1(n):
    g1 = n - 4
    return g1


print (guess1(5))
```

Reading 2

```
def guess2(n, m):
    g2 = n*m / 3
    return g2


print (guess2(5, 6))
```

Reading 3

```
def guess3(n, m):
    g3 = n *n + m
    return g3


print (guess3(3, 5))
```

5.5   Code Bloopers

Blooper 1

```
def power(n, power):
    a = n**p
    return a
```

```
print (power(5, 3))
print (power(8, 4))
print (power(9, 2))
```

Blooper 2

```
def cost(varcost, units, fixedcosts):
    costs = (varcost * units) + fixedcosts
    return costs
```

Blooper 3

```
def cost(varcost, units, fixedcost):
    costs = (varcost*units) + fixedcost
    return costs

print (costs(5, 10, 3))
```

Blooper 4

```
def power = (base, exponent):
    a = base**exponent
    return a

print(power(5, 3))
```

Blooper 5

```
def power(base, exponent):
a = base**exponent
return a
print (power(5,3))
```

Blooper 6

```
def to_the_power(n):
    out = n*4
    return out
```

5.6   Useful Built-in Functions

5.6.1   `lambda` Functions

`lambda` operator or `lambda` function is used for creating small, one-time and anonymous function objects in Python.

Anonymous means that they don't have a proper name, you just call them `lambda` functions. These functions come in handy when you need to do something on the fly or when you are working your way to solve a problem and you need additional resources to solve it. But you don't want to formally define them. For instance, you can call `lambda` functions inside a well defined functions to help you solving the problem. The syntax is very simple and goes as follows:

```
lambda <arguments>: <expression>
```

The `lambda` function can have any number of arguments, but it can have only one expression. In other words, we can have multiple parameters that we can pass in to the function but it has to do just one single operation. It cannot contain any statements and it returns a function object which can be assigned to any variable. Now you see why they cannot solve complex problems. You have to consider them as handy tools to help you solve the little chunks that belong to a bigger problem.

So let's define a formal function with name that computes the power of a number.

```
def give_me_power(n, p):
    return n**p

out = give_me_power(2, 2)
print(out)
## 4
```

Can we do the same operation with a `lambda` function?

```
my_lambda = lambda n, p: n**p

out = my_lambda(2, 2)
print(out)
## 4
```

As you can see, we get the same result and as confirmed by the chunk below, we also confirm that both the definitions lead to type `function`.

```
print(type(give_me_power) == type(my_lambda))
## True
print(type(my_lambda))
## <class 'function'>
```

Now, what if we wanted to do two operations? We just modify the function `give_me_power()` to make it add 10 to the result as follows:

```
def give_me_power(n, p):
    power = n**p
    out = power + 10
    return out

out = give_me_power(2, 2)
print(out)
## 14
```

```
my_lambda = lambda n, p: power = n**p; out = power + 10
# Simplify error output
## Error: can't assign to lambda
```

5.6.2   map() Function

map() function expects a function object and any number of iterables like lists, dictionaries, etc. The powerful thing is that you can pass to map() any function which will be then applied to the iterable. The function you pass will be executed for each element in the sequence and returns a type map. If you want to have your results, remember to cast map() to a list using list(). The syntax is as follows:

```
map(<function>, <iterable1>, <iterable2>, ...)
```

Let's say that we want to take the square root of a given sequence.

```
def give_me_sqrt(n):
    return n**0.5
```

```
my_map = map(give_me_sqrt, [_i for _i in range(11)])
print(my_map)
## <map object at 0x10f2bbfd0>
print(type(my_map))
## <class 'map'>
my_map_to_list = list(my_map)
for _i in my_map_to_list:
    print(_i)
## 0.0
## 1.0
## 1.4142135623730951
## 1.7320508075688772
```

```
## 2.0
## 2.23606797749979
## 2.449489742783178
## 2.6457513110645907
## 2.8284271247461903
## 3.0
## 3.1622776601683795
```

```
my_map = map(lambda x: x**0.5, [_i for _i in range(11)])
print(my_map)
## <map object at 0x10f2ab198>
print(type(my_map))
## <class 'map'>
my_map_to_list = list(my_map)
for _i in my_map_to_list:
    print(_i)
## 0.0
## 1.0
## 1.4142135623730951
## 1.7320508075688772
## 2.0
## 2.23606797749979
## 2.449489742783178
## 2.6457513110645907
## 2.8284271247461903
## 3.0
## 3.1622776601683795
```

5.6.3 `filter()` Function

`filter()` function expects two arguments, a function and an iterable. The function you passed returns a boolean value and it is called for each element of the iterable. `filter()` then returns only those element for which the function you passed returns True.

```
filter(<function>, <iterable>)
```

Please, remember that filter() accepts just one single iterable object.
So let's extract all the even numbers out of a sequence of numbers.

```
my_list = [_i for _i in range(11)]

my_filter = filter(lambda x: x % 2 == 0, my_list)
print(my_filter)
## <filter object at 0x10f2ba2b0>
print(type(my_filter))
## <class 'filter'>
my_filter_to_list = list(my_filter)
for _i in my_filter_to_list:
    print(_i)
## 0
## 2
## 4
## 6
## 8
## 10
```

5.7   Solutions to Code Bloopers

Blooper 1

We are using the parameter p instead of power.

Blooper 2

The colon : at the end of the first line is missing.

Blooper 3

We are printing the argument costs, but not the function cost.

Blooper 4

The = sign should not be in the function header.

Blooper 5

The function body must be indented.

Blooper 6

The correct operator is ** and not * which just multiplies two numbers.

5.8   Solutions to Exercises on Functions

Exercise 1

Create a function `square` that calculates the square of 5, 8, and 9

*HINT: You take the power of a number with the ** operator.*

Solution

```
def square(n):
    a = n**2
    return a

print (square(5))
## 25
print (square(8))
## 64
print (square(9))
## 81
```

Exercise 2

Create a function `power` that compute the p power of a number.

Then call this function to calculate:

- 5 to the power of 3;
- 8 to the power of 4;
- 9 to the power of 2.

Solution

```
def power(n,p):
    a = n**p
    return a

print (power(5,3))
## 125
print (power(8,4))
## 4096
print (power(9,2))
## 81
```

Exercise 3

Please calculate the cost of your Easter vacation by using the following inputs:

1. The trip lasts 4 nights and 5 days;
2. A night in the hotel costs $100;
3. The airplane ticket costs $300;
4. Renting a car costs $50 per day, and you will need a car for 5 days;
5. Each breakfast will cost $5 (5 breakfasts);
6. Each lunch will cost $20 (5 lunches);
7. Each dinner will cost $45 (5 dinners).

How much will you spend?

Solution

```
def hotel(hcost, nights):
    accomodation = hcost * nights
    return accomodation
def car(ccost, days):
    rental = ccost * days
```

```
    return rental
def eating(bcost, lcost, dcost, days):
    eat = (bcost + lcost + dcost) * days
    return eat
def vacation(hcost, nights, ccost, days,
             bcost, lcost, dcost, airfare):
    out = hotel(hcost, nights) + car(ccost, days) + \
          eating(bcost, lcost, dcost, days) + airfare
    return out

result = vacation(100, 4, 50, 5, 5, 20, 45, 300)
print(result)
## 1300
```

Chapter 6

Object Oriented Programming and Classes

One of the first concepts we mentioned at the very beginning of this book was Object Oriented Programming, or OOP. OOP is a fairly tough concept to understand especially for beginners. It is though absolutely important in order to fully exploit all Python capabilities.

6.1 Object Oriented Programming

What we have learned throughout the book was related to the creation of objects. We have seen that there exist several types of these objects and that each type comes with a set of pre-defined methods which we can use. What we are going to do in this chapter is to go behind the scenes to discover and understand what's beneath each object.

There are basically two things which we do not typically see in a front-end: the first one is some sort of data representation which tells Python how to represent the object and the second one tells us what are the ways we can interact with the object. Whenever we create an object we get three information about it:

1. the *type*;
2. an internal *data representation*;
3. an *interface* which defines a set of *procedures* (i.e. methods) for interacting with the object.

An object is an *instance* of a type so if we consider the number 1969 we say that this is an instance of an `int` type while `'Hello World'` is an instance of a `str` type.

Everything in Python is an object, including functions that we introduced in the previous chapter. An object has a particular type so we can create as many objects as we want with that type. We can manipulate these objects and we can also destroy them. A fundamental question we want to address in this chapter is: what are objects? In Python, objects are just a data abstraction which gathers some others information.

In order to better illustrate this concept, let's consider all the possible flight paths of the planes that land at and take-off from a given airport. First thing we probably note is the variability in the trajectories, but more importantly, we see planes coming in

in different colors, shapes, sizes and so on. In this example, the object is a plane. Now, let's focus on just one particular manufacturer that builds a particular type of plane. The manufacturer will probably have a blueprint of the plane or some sort of schematics which provides information about plane's attributes.

Going back to Python, a blueprint provides an internal representation of the object plane. From this, we can have general *representation data* as the length, the wingspan, the height, how many engines, how many seats and so on so forth. All this information tells us what data represents the plane.

Of course, we are also interested in how we can interact with the object. There are many ways: we can fly a plane, make it blue or red, switch on and off lights. This is part of the *interface* layer which tells us what methods are available to interact with the object.

Now let's move back to Python and try to apply these concepts. Consider an object L of type `list`. In particular, L = [1, 2, 3, 4]. We ask two questions: what is the data representation of a list? How do you interact and manipulate an object of type list? In Figure 6.1 we can see a representation of a list in Python. We note how this object is made up by two components:

1. boxes with values. For instance, at index zero, we have the value 1;
2. boxes with pointers represented by the symbol ->. Pointers tell Python where exactly is the memory location where you can access a given element of the list.

We basically observe that the representation of a list is just a chain of values and pointers.

FIGURE 6.1: Representation of an object of type list.

What we need to understand now is how do we interact with a list. Well, we already know this since we have been discussing it quite a lot in previous chapters. We know that when we have a list in Python, we can exploit several methods to manipulate it like the following:

- `L[i]`, `L[i:j]`, +;
- `len(L)`, `min(L)`, `max(L)`, `del(L[i])`;
- `L.append()`, `L.extend()`, `L.count()`, `L.index()`, `L.insert()`, `L.pop()`, `L.remove()`, `L.reverse()`, `L.sort()`.

So far, we explored the internals of objects, in particular lists. Why is this so important? Well, this is the beauty of OOP: we are not forced to know the internal representation of these methods as well as the data representation of the object itself. We do not need to know how these things have been coded. We just use them.

6.2   Classes

In this section we are going to go a little bit deeper. We want to know how an object can be crafted. With this, we are not referring to the simple creation of a given object with the assignment operator =. Here we will talk about the definition of the blueprint that provides the data representation as well as the related methods. We are introducing a new object which functions as an object constructor called *class*. The way we create classes resembles the one we introduced for functions.

One of the biggest advantages of OOP is the ability to bundle in one single entity called class both the data representation and the procedures which we can use to interact with an object that belongs to the defined class. Moreover, this way allows to write more general, more reusable and more readable codes in the future.

When we think about classes we really should think about two different steps. The first step should be dedicated in understanding and learning how to define a class. In other words, we want to know how to write a class. The second step should focus on how to use the defined class which in turns means how we access to the set of procedures defined in the class.

6.2.1   Writing a Class in Python

There are basically two steps we need to take care of when we want to first create a class:

1. define a class name. We recommend you to choose a meaningful name which resembles what the class represents or does;
2. define class attributes. Write all the methods associated with the class you defined which enable the interaction with the class itself.

After the class has been implemented, it is time to use it. Using a class implies that we can create new instances of objects which have our class name as type. Also, we can use the set of procedures and methods we wrote in the class to interact with objects belonging to that class. If we go back to the list shown in Figure 6.1, we know that someone has already created the class `list` and that this contains methods like `len(L)` to compute the number of elements in the list `L` or `L.append(5)` to append the number five at the end of the list `L`.

For the purpose of explaining how Python classes work, let's create a brand new class called `Person` which defines a set of attributes of a person. In order to do that, we need to use the reserved keyword `class` followed by the class name `Person` and a colon `:`. The initial code will look like the following:

```
class Person:
    '''This is the class Person'''
    # Put some attributes here
```

Please note that we used the triple quotes here. In the context of class definition, but also for functions, this is called *docstring*. The docstring serves as a specification on how a user should use the class.

After we defined the class, we can start putting attributes. These are the components of the class and define the data and the different procedures that belong only to our class, in this case `Person`. We can create as many attributes as we want. For this example, we want to keep things simple and just use, the first and last names, the age, and favorite rock band. These are the objects that are contained in the class, so for us they are the data that make up the class. Together with data, we have something else that you should already be aware of: methods. Methods are functions that only work with this class and they basically define the way we interact with objects belonging to the class.

6.2.2   The Special Method __init__()

Let's move on with the creation of the class `Person`. First thing we want to do is to define data attributes. In Python, we generally define attributes inside a class with a particular function called __init__()[1]. This is a *special method* which serves to initialize data attributes. The __init__() method is the first function which is dispatched (i.e. used) when we first create an object of type `Person`. Because it is the first function that gets executed, we put it right after the class initialization. Also, since it is a function, we use the reserved keyword `def` to create it and then we define the parameters we want to use in the function. In this case, these are the data attributes we want to attached to a person. So, the class gets populated as follows:

```
class Person:
    '''This is the class Person'''
    def __init__(self, first, last, age, band):
        self.first = first
        self.last  = last
        self.age   = age
        self.band  = band
```

As you can see, we have our four parameters that describe a person but we also have another parameter named `self`. This parameter needs a bit of attention since this is the way we tell Python how we want to access to the object's properties inside the method. If you noted, when we define the different parameters we always use the standard notation of `self.`. So when we invoke `self.first` we are saying: look at the data attribute `first` that belongs to the class `Person`[2]. So remember, for methods that belong to the class, the first parameter is always going

---

[1] __init__() is sometimes called the object's constructor, because it mimics the way that constructors are used in other languages. For technical reasons, this is not entirely correct. It is better to call it the *initializer*.

[2] The fact that we are using `self.first` to be assign to the parameter `first` is

to be `self`[3]. All the other parameters specify what data initializes the object `Person`.

One question could be asked here: how do we make sure that those parameters are of the correct types? This is a fair legitimate question and we are going to answer in two ways:

1. you can clearly explain what type each and every parameter must be in the docstring. You can also warn the user that any deviation from what is suggested might lead to unintended or unexpected behaviors;
2. you can explicitly write *asserts* in the `__init__()` method to enforce the use of correct types.

6.2.3   Adding More Methods

What we are about to do now is to add some others features to our class. In particular, we have a parameter for the age of the person, but we do not know right away the year of birth. So let's define another function which implements this very simple transformation. What we need to do is to add the new function called `year_of_birth()` below the method `__init__()` as follows:

```
class Person:
    '''This is the class Person'''
    def __init__(self, first, last, age = None, band = None):
        self.first = first
        self.last  = last
        self.age   = age
        self.band  = band
```

---

not mandatory. We can change the name of the data attribute though we recommend to use the same names for better readability and interpretability of the code.

[3]The name `self` is a convention. You can call this parameter the way you want, but we strongly recommend to stick with the Python naming convention.

```
def year_of_birth(self, current_year):
    self.current_year = current_year
    yob = self.current_year - self.age
    return yob
```

Please note how we refer to the age of the person using `self.age`. This is because `age` is a defined attribute in the class `Person`.

6.2.4   Creating and Using a Class

It is now time to use the class and create an object of class `Person`. In this case, we are creating an object call `franz` with the following attributes:

```
franz = Person(
    'Francesco',
    'Grossetti',
    35,
    'Pink Floyd'
)


# we want to check the type
print(type(franz))
## <class '__main__.Person'>
```

This instruction executes the `__init__()` method we defined. As you can see, when we print the type we get a different message now which does not completely resemble what we were accustomed to. Without going into too many details, the reason why we get this message and not just the name of the class is because we did not define some components in the class. If we want to get a cleaner message, we can specify the following instruction:

```
print(type(franz).__name__)
## Person
```

The object **franz** has all the attributes we defined in __init__(). We can access to the attributes with the usual dot operator as follows:

```
print(franz.first)
## Francesco
print(franz.last)
## Grossetti
print(franz.age)
## 35
print(franz.band)
## Pink Floyd
```

Before we move on, there are few things worth noting. Firstly (1), even if we set a parameter named **self**, we do not use it explicitly when we call **Person**. The reason is due to the fact that Python automatically manages this parameter by assigning it to the object we are defining, in this case **franz**. All we have to specify then are the remaining four parameters. Secondly (2), we naturally respect the order of the parameters in __init__(). This sounds trivial, but could lead to bugs and errors. Since we are the creators of the class **Person**, we know exactly what's inside __init__() and we know the order in the parameters definition. To show you how this could lead to issues, let's define another object **franz2** in which we change the order of the first and last names. We then access to the attributes **first** and **last** to check their values.

```
franz2 = Person(
    'Grossetti',
    'Francesco',
    35,
```

```
    'Pink Floyd'
)


# This should be the first name, but it's not!
print(franz2.first)
# This should be the last name, but it's not!
## Grossetti
print(franz2.last)
## Francesco
```

So, how do we solve this issue? What if we want to specify a different order just because we like it more or it is just easier for us to remember? Well, it's very simple, we use =. Let's define `franz2` again by putting last name in the first place:

```
franz2 = Person(
    last  = 'Grossetti',
    first = 'Francesco',
    age   = 35,
    band  = 'Pink Floyd'
)


# This should be the first name, and it is!
print(franz2.first)
## Francesco
print(franz2.first)
# This should be the last name, and it is!
## Francesco
print(franz2.last)
## Grossetti
```

If you remember, we also defined a method called `year_of_birth()` which takes a single parameter and computes the person's year of birth according to the specified `age`. The way we use this method once again is with the dot operator:

```
print(franz2.year_of_birth(2018))
## 1983
```

6.2.5   Class Inheritance

At this point of the book, we should all be aware of the incredible potential of Python. In particular with classes, we understood how we can generate an object with specific properties and pre-defined methods to interact with.

When we created the class `Person` we were probably thinking about giving a quick and general description of a person. What we want to do in this Section is to go a bit deeper and introduce the concept of *inheritance*. Inheritance means that a given entity possesses the same attributes of another entity. If we re-think this concept in terms of Python classes, when we create another object of class `Person`, say `gaia`, this object will have the same attributes as the object `franz`. Please note that we are not talking about values. Values are going to be different because they are what make a person different from another.

6.2.5.1   Parent Classes

The concept of inheritance goes along with *parent* and *child classes*[4]. As the name suggests, parent classes create a pattern out of which child classes can be based on. For example, the class `Person` is a parent class. We define parent classes by simply using `class` and a name for that class. We know that we have a `__init__()` method and, in principle, other methods as well.

---

[4]Sometimes parent and child classes are called base classes and sub-classes, respectively.

6.2.5.2   Child Classes

Suppose that we want to include information about what type of job a person does. we can either include the job type as an attribute in the parent class `Person` or, more appropriately, we can define a child class `Occupation` which instantiates some methods based on the job we specify. Child classes inherit all the attributes of parent class, but they can implement new methods as well. Intuitively, we understand how a pilot would have a method called `flying()`, while a teacher could have a method called `teaching()`.

Let's start by creating a child class of `Person` called `Occupation` with no additional methods. This means that `Occupation` inherits all the methods of `Person`. To define a child class which inherits all the attributes and the methods of its parent, we simply put the name of the parent class in parenthesis and inside the scope, we just declare `pass`. Look at the example below where we define the child class `Occupation` which inherits from `Person`.

```
class Occupation(Person):
    pass
```

To check that `Occupation` really inherited all the attributes, we simply invoke them without using `Person` class.

```
new_person = Occupation(
    first = 'Miles',
    last  = 'Davis',
    age   = 58,
    band  = 'myself'
)

print(type(new_person))
## <class '__main__.Occupation'>
```

```
print(new_person.first)
## Miles
```

What is really powerful is that we can add new attributes and methods independently to child classes. The class `Occupation` seems to be a bit too general for our purposes. For instance, let's consider a teacher and a commercial pilot. They clearly have very different occupations, so what we would like to do is to add specific attributes and/or methods for these two new classes.

To add attributes and methods to a class, we proceed similarly to what we did for the class `Person`. Let's start with the teacher's class:

```
class Teacher(Person):
    '''This is the class Teacher'''
    def __init__(self, n_students, n_classes,
                 n_hours_week, subject,
                 first, last, age = None, band = None):
        self.n_students   = n_students
        self.n_classes    = n_classes
        self.n_hours_week = n_hours_week
        self.subject      = subject
        super().__init__(first, last, age, band)

    def avg_n_student_per_class(self):
        out = self.n_students / self.n_classes
        return out
    def avg_n_hours_per_week(self, n_days):
        self.n_days = n_days
        out = self.n_hours_week / self.n_days
        return out
```

For this class, we added four more attributes: `n_students`, `n_classes`, `n_hours_week`, and `subject`. These all describe the specific job of a teacher by providing information on the number of students and the number of classes the teacher have, the number of working hours per week and the subject that the teacher teaches. In addition, we have two methods: `avg_n_student_per_class()` and `avg_n_hours_per_week()` which computes the average number of students per class and the average number of working hours per day.

Now we create a class for a commercial pilot and we call it `Pilot`. We add in attributes for the number of passengers, the scheduled number of hours that the pilot has to fly for a given week, the total number of hours the pilot flew in his/her career and the type of plane he/she flies.

```
class Pilot(Person):
    '''This is the class Pilot'''
    def __init__(self, n_passengers, scheduled_hours,
                 total_hours, plane,
                 first, last, age = None, band = None):
        self.n_passengers    = n_passengers
        self.scheduled_hours = scheduled_hours
        self.total_hours     = total_hours
        self.plane           = plane
        super().__init__(first, last, age, band)

    def compute_total_hours(self):
        out = self.scheduled_hours + self.total_hours
        return out
```

6.2.5.3   The `super()` Function

Before creating two instances for these new classes, it is important to note this specific line of code which we find in the two definitions of our child classes:

```
super().__init__(first, last, age, band)
```

This line basically tells Python to add the parent class __init__()
attributes to the child class too. In other words, with the super() function
we can gain access to inherited methods that have been overwritten
in a class object. The super() function is typically used within the
__init__() method. In fact, here is the place where we would like to add
specific behaviors of child classes and then we complete the initialization
from the parent class using the super() function.

When we use the super() function, we are invoking a method or
attributes which has been defined in the parent class into a child class.
This is very useful and powerful and allows to generalize the code even
more. The most intuitive use is to override one aspect of the parent class
and maybe add or just modify a given functionality. At the same time,
we want to be sure we can call all the original methods.

In the examples above, we added some descriptors for the parent
class Person by defining two child classes, Teacher and Pilot, with their
specific attributes and methods but retaining the original attributes of
the parent class. Let's apply everything then:

```
a_teacher = Teacher(
  first = 'Richard',
  last  = 'Feynman',
  subject = 'Physics',
  n_hours_week = 30,
  n_students = 100,
  n_classes = 10
)

print(a_teacher.avg_n_student_per_class())
## 10.0
```

```
print(a_teacher.avg_n_hours_per_week(4))
## 7.5
```

```
a_pilot = Pilot(
  first = 'Amelia',
  last  = 'Earhart',
  age = 40,
  n_passengers = 2,
  scheduled_hours = 100,
  total_hours = 1000,
  plane = 'Lockeed L-10 Electra'
)
```

```
print(a_pilot.n_passengers)
## 2
print(a_pilot.scheduled_hours)
## 100
print(a_pilot.total_hours)
## 1000
print(a_pilot.compute_total_hours())
## 1100
```

Chapter 7

Python Modules: pandas

One of the most important features of Python is that it comes with plenty of additional libraries which can be used to solve specific tasks. These libraries are called *modules* and their aim is to add features to base Python. In this chapter, you will learn how to install, import and work with new modules. We will also focus on one specific and very important module called `pandas`.

7.1 Installing and Importing a Module

Since a module is just an additional software, before we can use it, we need to make it available in the system. In other words, we need to install it. There are basically two ways to do this[1]:

1. install it via `pip` with the command:

```
pip install "module_name"
```

2. install it via Anaconda using virtual environments. To know a little

---

[1]Please, note that the quotation marks are not required in the commands below.

bit more about virtual environments we suggest this guide[2]. Once
the environment has been created, simply install the module with:

```
conda install "module_name"
```

Once the modules have been installed in your system, you can load
them in Python by invoking the command `import`. There are some
conventions in the naming which we encourage you to follow. For example,
a well known module for scientific computing is `numpy`. Typically, we
import it as follows:

```
import numpy as np
```

As you can see, we added the keyword `as` and then we specified a shorter
name as `np`. This allows us to access to `numpy` methods by simply calling
`np.my_method()` instead of calling `numpy.my_method()`. In other words,
this is just a less verbose way to access to features within a given module.

7.2   Managing Databases With Pandas

One of the most important tasks the we have to carry out on a daily
basis is the management of databases. Databases can come in all sort of
structures. Typical file extensions are Microsoft Excel, or *.csv* (i.e. comma
separated values) files. These types of files are very handy since they
have a rectangular structure in which we have observations in rows and
features in columns.

In Python, there is a incredibly powerful module which has been
conceived to process and manipulate rectangular data structures called
`pandas`. `pandas` is well maintained and you can find lots of tutorials and
resources online. We suggest to start at https://pandas.pydata.org. What

---

[2]https://docs.python-guide.org/dev/virtualenvs/#lower-level-virtualenv.

we would like to do is being able to import an Excel file into Python
and process it with pandas. Before we start this, we have to import the
required modules as follows:

```
import pandas as pd
import numpy as np
```

As you can see, we imported both pandas masked as pd and numpy
masked as np. Since we will explore data, we would also like to do
some visualizations. One of the most common modules for graphics is
matplotlib. Hence, we import it as follows:

```
# Plot libraries
from matplotlib import patheffects
import matplotlib.pyplot as plt
# the line below configures some
# plotting parameters
plt.rcParams["figure.figsize"] = (12,12)
```

As you can tell, here we used another keyword which is from. In
this way, we explicitly tell Python the exact method we want to make
available. In the example above, we are saying that from the whole
matplotlib module, we just want patheffects. We also import the
method matplotlib.pyplot and we mask it with the conventional name
plt.

7.2.1   Import External Files as Data Frames

We are now ready to physically import an external file into the Python
environment. pandas is able to ready from a variety of different file formats
like CSV, Excel, SQL. The module comes with built-in methods to read
in data specifically designed to work with the different file formats. The
general syntax to import a file is as follows:

```
# For CSV files
df_csv = pd.read_csv('path/to/file.csv')


# For Excel files
df_excel = pd.read_excel('path/to/file.xlsx')


# For SQL files
df_sql = pd.read_sql("SELECT * FROM table", con)
```

Please note that when we read in a SQL database, we have to have a valid and active connections which we named `con`. One way to define a connection to a database is through the module `sqlite3` as follows:

```
con = sqlite3.connect('my_sql_db')
```

Now that you are more familiar with Python, it is easier to understand the syntax. Even if we are using a module, `pandas`, we can see that we call functions (i.e. methods) belonging to the module with the usual dot operator `.`. So writing `pd.read_csv('path/to/file.csv')` call the function `read_csv()` contained in `pandas` which allows us to import a .csv file. The string `'path/to/file.csv'` represents the location of the file we want to import on the local drive. The example we are going to use is a csv file. In order to import it we have to use the `pd.read_csv()` function as follows:

```
df = pd.read_csv("data/twitter_lockout.csv")
```

We now have an object of type `Data.Frame` named `df`. `Data.Frame`(s) are the typical objects which you are going to use on a daily basis. You can find them in almost every programming languages and they are typically called *data.frame*(s). So whenever we refer to a `pandas` object, we immediately know that this object will be of type `Data.Frame`.

As you can imagine, there are plenty of operations we can carry out on this object. For instance, we can now have look at the data with the function `head()`, which by default displays just the first 5 rows in our database. Just remember: a `Data.Frame` assumes we have observations in rows and features in columns. If you want to display a different number of rows, just specify the number you want as an argument as follows[3]:

```
# defeault 5 rows
df.head())
```

date	tweetsent	followers	retweet
2018-02-21 15:40:58	8999	722	0
2018-02-21 15:40:58	48791	634	662
2018-02-21 15:40:57	17585	6525	586
2018-02-21 15:40:57	13178	178	84
2018-02-21 15:40:57	5421	554	199
2018-02-21 15:40:57	48595	3616	1749

Or just the first two rows:

```
df.head(2))
```

date	tweetsent	followers	retweet
2018-02-21 15:40:58	8999	722	0
2018-02-21 15:40:58	48791	634	662

One could be interested in looking at the bottom rows. In order to do so, you can use the function `tail()`. As you probably guessed, by default `tail()` display the bottom 5 rows, so once again, you can specify a custom number as an argument of the function. For instance, let us display the bottom 2 rows:

---

[3]Please note that the `print()` function is used here just to ensure the correct output. When working with `pandas` functions like `head()` or `tail()` automatically displays the information. In other words, the `print()` function is not strictly required.

```
df.tail(3)
```

date	tweetsent	followers	retweet
2018-02-21 17:24:19	83199	2315	35
2018-02-21 17:24:19	51889	653	444
2018-02-21 17:24:19	1687	90	0

7.3   Indexing

Let us now learn how to identify specific columns or rows in a data frame. In other words, we want to apply the so called *indexing*. Indexing is helpful, we should say fundamental to perform any operation on columns or rows.

7.3.1   Columns

The first thing we want to do is to understand what columns are in our Data.Frame object. We simply use the columns method, without parenthesis[4].

```
df.columns
## Index(['hndl', 'date', 'tweetsent', 'followers', 'retweet'],
##    dtype='object')
```

We can also put all the columns into a list, should we need it, with tolist().

---

[4]The fact that to call this method we do not have to use the usual parenthesis is out of the scope of this book. You will learn that some functions require them, other do not.

```
df.columns.tolist()
## ['hndl', 'date', 'tweetsent', 'followers', 'retweet']
```

After seeing the columns in our data frame, let us learn how to select just one column. Similarly to what we did to access elements in lists, we can access columns with a square bracket []. With lists, we indicate each element with its index. In data frames, we indicate each column with its name. Thus, to access the column followers we would write:

```
df['followers']
## 0         722
## 1         634
## 2        6525
## 3         178
## 4         554
## 5        3616
## 6           6
## 7         188
## 8        4813
## 9        2978
## 10        535
## 11         62
## 12        361
## 13      15044
## 14      12537
## 15        268
## 16        626
## 17        195
## 18        751
## 19      97781
## 20       2089
## 21       3973
## 22        294
```

```
## 23          813
## 24          482
## 25         1423
## 26         1125
## 27         3148
## 28        11512
## 29          498
##             ...
## 46361        105
## 46362         12
## 46363       1091
## 46364       3337
## 46365        253
## 46366      10441
## 46367       1264
## 46368        106
## 46369         10
## 46370        340
## 46371       1497
## 46372       1400
## 46373        121
## 46374        767
## 46375        179
## 46376       2955
## 46377        282
## 46378        319
## 46379       1900
## 46380       1883
## 46381       2677
## 46382       2523
## 46383        250
## 46384        331
```

```
## 46385        806
## 46386        439
## 46387         93
## 46388       2315
## 46389        653
## 46390         90
## Name: followers, Length: 46391, dtype: int64
```

We are not going to print it because it would be a very long list. However, remember that you can always slice columns in the same way as we sliced lists. For instance, we can access the first 3 rows of the column **followers** as:

```
df['followers'][:3]
## 0       722
## 1       634
## 2      6525
## Name: followers, dtype: int64
```

Alternatively, you can treat the name like an attribute of the data frame **df** and use a dot operator to access a column, like this:

```
df.followers
## 0        722
## 1        634
## 2       6525
## 3        178
## 4        554
## 5       3616
## 6          6
## 7        188
## 8       4813
## 9       2978
```

```
## 10         535
## 11          62
## 12         361
## 13       15044
## 14       12537
## 15         268
## 16         626
## 17         195
## 18         751
## 19       97781
## 20        2089
## 21        3973
## 22         294
## 23         813
## 24         482
## 25        1423
## 26        1125
## 27        3148
## 28       11512
## 29         498
##           . . .
## 46361      105
## 46362       12
## 46363     1091
## 46364     3337
## 46365      253
## 46366    10441
## 46367     1264
## 46368      106
## 46369       10
## 46370      340
## 46371     1497
```

```
## 46372        1400
## 46373         121
## 46374         767
## 46375         179
## 46376        2955
## 46377         282
## 46378         319
## 46379        1900
## 46380        1883
## 46381        2677
## 46382        2523
## 46383         250
## 46384         331
## 46385         806
## 46386         439
## 46387          93
## 46388        2315
## 46389         653
## 46390          90
## Name: followers, Length: 46391, dtype: int64
```

Are we sure that the two notations yield the same output? Let us check!

```
text1 = df['followers']
text2 = df.followers

# check whether the Series are the same
print(text1 is text2)
## True
```

Let us now see what type of object we have created:

```
print(type(text1))
## <class 'pandas.core.series.Series'>
print(type(text2))
## <class 'pandas.core.series.Series'>
```

As you can see, we have created an object called `Series`. We can convert this `Series` to a list with the usual function `tolist()` as we have done before to put the names of the columns in a list

```
followers_list = df['followers'].tolist()
print(type(followers_list))
## <class 'list'>
```

We might be interested in doing something more than just selecting more than one column. In order to do that, we need to pass the names of the columns we are interested in as a list:

```
df2 = df[['date','tweetsent']]
df2.head(2)
##                    date   tweetsent
## 0  2018-02-21 15:40:58        8999
## 1  2018-02-21 15:40:58       48791
```

date	tweetsent
2018-02-21 15:40:58	8999
2018-02-21 15:40:58	48791

Please note that the first `[]` allows the access to the data frame, while the second `[]` allows you to select the columns. This selection returns another `Data.Frame` object. To select more than one column, we can use the first method only. This makes sense since the dot operator makes a direct link with that very column you specified and it won't allow any other specifications.

After all these operations, one thing has been left over: what is the size of this data? In other words, how many rows and columns are in your data frame? One thing to note is that there is an extra column at the very beginning of our data frame, which does not come from the original csv file that we uploaded. This initial column is called `index` and it is a fixed `ID` that identifies each row of the data frame. This index is created by default by `pandas` the minute we import a data set. Whatever operations we carry out on our data frame, the index will never change. The only way we have to access this column is through the dot operator.

The simplest way to know how many observations are in a column, we can ask its length with the usual function `len()` as follows:

```
print(len(df.index))
## 46391
print(len(df["followers"]))
## 46391
```

As we pointed out before, the following code will return an error since we are trying to access the column `index` using a list.

```
print(len(df["index"]))
```

Indeed, there is no column called `index`.

7.3.1.1 Series functions

We can of course analyze a `Series` object. For instance, we can get some descriptive with `describe()` by once again using the usual dot operation. The intuition here is to just *chain* the instructions one after another one. In the following chunk, you can see how first we select the column `retweet` and then (i.e. with .) we ask for its description.

```
print(df["retweet"].describe())
## count      46391.000000
## mean         881.653036
## std         1502.878469
## min            0.000000
## 25%            6.000000
## 50%          234.000000
## 75%          870.000000
## max         7060.000000
## Name: retweet, dtype: float64
```

You could also call one specific descriptive with the corresponding function, e.g., count(), mean(), max() or min().

```
print(df["retweet"].max())
## 7060
```

7.3.2   Rows

Retrieving a row is also possible, but we have to use a different method called iloc. This method requires the exact row number as input. For instance,

```
print(df2.iloc[2])
## date            2018-02-21 15:40:57
## tweetsent                    17585
## Name: 2, dtype: object
```

Alternatively, you can use the loc method. While iloc is primarily integer position based, loc is primarily label based.

```
print(df2.loc[2])
## date        2018-02-21 15:40:57
## tweetsent                 17585
## Name: 2, dtype: object
```

7.4 Adding new columns

We can create new columns in the same way we create objects in Python.

```
df["name_of_the_column"] = <instructions here>
```

Let's create a column called `reach` that is the ratio between the number of re-tweets and number of followers. We can do it by just accessing the two columns we are interested in and computing the ratio:

```
df["reach"] = df["retweet"] / df["followers"]
```

To check what we have done, let us print just the first 5 rows of the columns `followers`, `retweet`, and `reach`. First, we pass the three columns we want to access as a list:

```
df[["followers","retweet", "reach"]]
##       followers  retweet        reach
## 0           722        0     0.000000
## 1           634      662     1.044164
## 2          6525      586     0.089808
## 3           178       84     0.471910
## 4           554      199     0.359206
## 5          3616     1749     0.483684
## 6             6     4589   764.833333
## 7           188     4589    24.409574
```

```
## 8           4813       124     0.025764
## 9           2978         0     0.000000
## 10           535      4424     8.269159
## 11            62       340     5.483871
## 12           361         4     0.011080
## 13         15044         1     0.000066
## 14         12537         0     0.000000
## 15           268      1320     4.925373
## 16           626        10     0.015974
## 17           195         1     0.005128
## 18           751         0     0.000000
## 19         97781         0     0.000000
## 20          2089       728     0.348492
## 21          3973       626     0.157564
## 22           294         0     0.000000
## 23           813         1     0.001230
## 24           482      1683     3.491701
## 25          1423      2269     1.594519
## 26          1125       223     0.198222
## 27          3148       229     0.072745
## 28         11512         0     0.000000
## 29           498         0     0.000000
## ...           ...       ...          ...
## 46361        105         0     0.000000
## 46362         12      1115    92.916667
## 46363       1091        13     0.011916
## 46364       3337        24     0.007192
## 46365        253      1115     4.407115
## 46366      10441         1     0.000096
## 46367       1264      1499     1.185918
## 46368        106      1115    10.518868
## 46369         10      1242   124.200000
```

```
## 46370         340        2733    8.038235
## 46371        1497          77    0.051436
## 46372        1400         625    0.446429
## 46373         121          24    0.198347
## 46374         767           0    0.000000
## 46375         179         973    5.435754
## 46376        2955        1248    0.422335
## 46377         282         858    3.042553
## 46378         319           0    0.000000
## 46379        1900         118    0.062105
## 46380        1883         981    0.520977
## 46381        2677         283    0.105715
## 46382        2523         941    0.372969
## 46383         250         444    1.776000
## 46384         331           0    0.000000
## 46385         806         273    0.338710
## 46386         439           2    0.004556
## 46387          93           2    0.021505
## 46388        2315          35    0.015119
## 46389         653         444    0.679939
## 46390          90           0    0.000000
##
## [46391 rows x 3 columns]
```

Then, select the first 5 rows. You have four options here:

```
# option 1
print(df[["followers","retweet", "reach"]].head(5))
##    followers  retweet      reach
## 0        722        0   0.000000
## 1        634      662   1.044164
## 2       6525      586   0.089808
## 3        178       84   0.471910
```

```
## 4          554          199  0.359206
```

```
# option 2
print(df[["followers","retweet", "reach"]][:5])
##     followers  retweet     reach
## 0          722        0  0.000000
## 1          634      662  1.044164
## 2         6525      586  0.089808
## 3          178       84  0.471910
## 4          554      199  0.359206
```

```
# option 3
print(df[["followers","retweet", "reach"]].loc[5])
## followers      3616.000000
## retweet        1749.000000
## reach             0.483684
## Name: 5, dtype: float64
```

```
# option 4
print(df[["followers","retweet", "reach"]].iloc[5])
## followers      3616.000000
## retweet        1749.000000
## reach             0.483684
## Name: 5, dtype: float64
```

Now, let us create another column named `author_followership`, which is a categorical variable to indicate the size of each author's followership as follows:

- *small*: if the number of followers is below the average;
- *big*: otherwise.

First, we need to figure out the mean number of followers. How? Well, we access the column `followers` and then ask for its mean with the function `Series.mean()`.

```
avg_followers = df["followers"].mean()
print(avg_followers)
## 4412.800694100149
```

Then, we apply the function `pd.cut()` to the column `followers`. This function has three main arguments:

- `x`: the input array to bin
- `bins`: the criteria to bin by (i.e, the bin edges);
- `labels`: specifies the labels for the returned bins.

We first store our `bins` and `labels` in two separate lists. Then, we apply `pd.cut()` to the column `followers` as follows:

```
bins   = [0, avg_followers, np.inf]
labels = ['small', 'big']
df['author_followership'] = pd.cut(x = df['followers'],
                                   bins = bins,
                                   labels = labels)
```

7.5 Working with dates

`pandas` has a nice built-in method to work with date: `datetime`. First, we create a new column `date1` that convert our column `date` into a `datetime` format:

```
df["date1"] = pd.to_datetime(df["date"])
```

Then, we can create columns containing the year, month, day, and even minutes and seconds, with the function `Series.dt()`:

```
df['year']    = df['date1'].dt.year
df['month']   = df['date1'].dt.month
df['day']     = df['date1'].dt.day
df['hour']    = df['date1'].dt.hour
df['minute']  = df['date1'].dt.minute
df['second']  = df['date1'].dt.second
```

Now let's explore the new structure:

```
# calling a head
df.head()
```

date1	year	month	day	hour	minute	second
2018-02-21 15:40:58	2018	2	21	15	40	58
2018-02-21 15:40:58	2018	2	21	15	40	58
2018-02-21 15:40:57	2018	2	21	15	40	57
2018-02-21 15:40:57	2018	2	21	15	40	57
2018-02-21 15:40:57	2018	2	21	15	40	57

7.6   Grouping

We can group our data according to the value of one column with the function `groupby()`. It takes as an argument the name of the column we want to use to group our data.

```
df.groupby(column_name)
```

Just using `groupby()` creates a `groupby.DataFrameGroupBy` object. To obtain a specific statistics, we need to specify it after `groupby()`. These are just some of the possibilities:

- `sum()`

- `count()`
- `mean()`
- `median()`
- `min()`
- `max()`

For instance, each *hour*, we can compute the mean of each numeric column in our data frame with the function `mean()`.

```
df.groupby('hour').mean()
```

hour	tweetsent	followers	retweet	year	month	day	minute
15	41961.59	3823.360	800.4740	2018	2	21	19.61791
14	40949.40	4020.037	990.1922	2018	2	21	42.27292
17	42195.12	5812.437	864.4247	2018	2	21	41.53195

Now, let us have a look at the authors who wrote the most tweets. We use the function `Series.value_counts()` that returns the number of times each author posted a tweet.

```
counts = df["hndl"].value_counts()
print(type(counts))
## <class 'pandas.core.series.Series'>
```

The object `counts` that we just created is basically a pandas `Series` with one column that contains the number of tweets each author posted. The index is the name of the author. We can print it in the same way we print a data frame:

```
print(counts.head())
## rhoho1118        62
## MulfacASMR       48
## redrevcorp       48
```

```
## honeybunchesof8      37
## rentonMagaUK         36
## Name: hndl, dtype: int64
```

If we want to print the percentages instead of the absolute numbers, we can just passing `normalize=True` as an argument of `value_counts`.

```
counts = df["hndl"].value_counts(normalize=True)
print(counts.head())
## rhoho1118           0.001336
## MulfacASMR          0.001035
## redrevcorp          0.001035
## honeybunchesof8     0.000798
## rentonMagaUK        0.000776
## Name: hndl, dtype: float64
```

7.7   Exercises on Pandas

Exercise 1

Print the first four rows of the columns `followers` and `author_followership`.

7.8   Solutions to Exercises on Pandas

Solution to Exercise 1

Solution 1

```
print(df[["followers", "author_followership"]][:4])
##    followers author_followership
## 0        722               small
## 1        634               small
## 2       6525                 big
## 3        178               small
```

Solution 2

```
print(df[["followers", "author_followership"]].loc[:4])
##     followers author_followership
## 0        722               small
## 1        634               small
## 2       6525                 big
## 3        178               small
## 4        554               small
```

Solution 3

```
print(df[["followers", "author_followership"]].iloc[:4])
##     followers author_followership
## 0        722               small
## 1        634               small
## 2       6525                 big
## 3        178               small
```